Power LINUX

D1322790

Springer

Berlin
Heidelberg
New York
Barcelona
Budapest
Hong Kong
London
Milan
Paris
Santa Clara
Singapore
Tokyo

Stefan Probst and Ralf Flaxa are qualified computer scientists. During their studies at the University of Erlangen-Nürnberg they acquired extensive knowledge in the field of UNIX and networks, and since 1992 they have taken an active part in the development of Linux. They formed the Linux Support Team and developed the free LST distribution. With this and the system tool LISA (Linux Installation and System Administration) they have made a worldwide name for themselves in the Linux field. They have also developed Linux systems and software for Caldera in the USA.

Stefan Probst   Ralf Flaxa

Power LINUX
Linux 2.0 – LST-Distribution 2.2

With 57 Figures and 2 CD-ROMs

 Springer

Authors
Stefan Probst, Ralf Flaxa
LST-Software, Lazarettstr. 8
D-91054 Erlangen, Germany

Translators
Antje Faber
Gerhart-Hauptmann-Str. 19
D-91058 Erlangen, Germany

Roger Pook
Budapester Str. 16
D-91056 Erlangen, Germany

Library of Congress Cataloging-in-Publication Data
Probst, Stefan, 1967-
  The power Linux: Linux 2.0, LST-distribution 2.2/Stefan Probst,
Ralf Flaxa
    p.   cm.
    ISBN 3-540-14556-7
    1. Linux. 2. Operating systems (Computers)   I. Flaxa, Ralf,
1968-   . II. Title.
QA76.76.063P758   1997
005.4´469--dc20   97-6927
                                                   CIP

ISBN 3-540-14556-7 Springer-Verlag Berlin Heidelberg New York

© Springer-Verlag Berlin Heidelberg 1997
Printed in Germany

Typesetting: Camera ready by the authors and Fred Hantelmann, Hamburg
Cover design: Künkel + Lopka, Heidelberg
SPIN 10527216   Printed on acid-free paper   33/3142 – 5 4 3 2 1 0

Contents

Contents

Introduction

1.1 The Linux Operating System

The question, dear reader, is where to start a book with the intention of giving an overview of the fascinating world of Linux? Perhaps it should begin with something about Linux and its history.

No other software project has in such a short time developed into such a comprehensive and stable system. Perhaps the most amazing part of the story is the way in which the system has reached such a high standard. Completely lacking the usual time pressure and without any requirement documents thousands of hobby programmers worldwide, in contact with each other only via the internet, have produced an operating system which is incomparable in its stability, functionality, and openness.

Unique development

Openness means that the complete source code is freely available and the system can be extended through common interfaces. No other operating system development is as open for additions and performance improvement as Linux. NetBSD comes close, but its design is controlled by a relatively closed group of developers.

The strengths: openness, stability, functionality and performance

It is stable because there are even computers which ran for over a year without a single crash using the early versions before Linux 1.0. Misbehaving programs very rarely bring Linux to a standstill, unlike other PC operating systems. Linux is designed to provide uninterrupted operation. Linux is also stable in another sense. Its basic design principles are very unlikely to change from year to year. We can say this with confidence as Linux's role model, Unix, has been in existence since 1969 and in the last 27 years has only been improved.

It is functional because you can get most of the same software that is known and cherished in the Unix world for Linux. On most hardware platforms, Linux is a 32 bit operating system. Linux even brings impressive performance back to an old 386SX processor. At the other end of the scale, 64 bit Linux for the DEC Alpha and various symetric multi-processor Linux versions gives top-class performance.

*New concepts
and methods*

The price for all this convenience is that one may have to set aside the habits acquired from using other PC operating systems and come to terms with new concepts and procedures. You will probably enjoy forgetting the old habit of pressing the reset button to cure software problems. Discovering how well you can work with multitasking and multiple virtual terminals will undoubtedly be a real joy. You may be a little shy about programming now, but once you have seen how much you can achieve with a simple one line script program you'll be hooked. Linux provides exactly the right environment for becoming familiar with these concepts. Your investment is a little bit of time and the willingness to learn. Your reward is a great deal of fun and personal growth as you become more familiar with Linux.

1.1.1 The Performance Capabilities of Linux

Surely you have already heard of the many faceted benefits of Linux. We can list the most significant advantages so that you understand why one sees "Linux Inside" (Fig. 1.1) on PCs more and more often.

Fig. 1.1: Does your computer already have "Linux Inside"?

*Real 32 bit
multiuser
multitasking
operating system*

- 32 bit multiuser multitasking operating system, therefore all programs are available exclusively as real 32 bit applications which utilise the features of the processor to the limit. The system works with real, pre-emptive multitasking, providing each individual process with its own virtual processor. In practice this means that several users can work on one computer simultaneously and that every one of them can use several programs at the same time, without one of them being favoured or the programs interfering with each other.[1]

*Complete
network
function*

- Complete network support based on the internet TCP/IP protocol, which means you can connect several Linux computers simply and share the resources (performance, hard disk space) of all computers within the network transparently.

---

[1] Naturally that applies only so long as the processor load is less than 100%. Under high system loads not even Unix can extract more computing performance.

- Linux recognizes almost all common file systems and can work with at least 12 of them. It is therefore possible to get access to the data of other operating systems. This is particularly useful when you want to use a heterogeneous network of DOS and Unix computers.

- Graphical interface with XFree86 X Window system, providing the actual X11R6.1 interface from MIT. X11 is the standard graphical interface of Unix, providing network-wide use of graphical resources transparently. This means you can call up the screen outputs (the windows) of an application from every computer on the network, regardless of which computer actually runs the program. In this fashion you can use applications running on other Unix computers (for example on a SUN Workstation).

  X Window graphical interface system

- Comprehensive software development platform which provides the GNU gcc compiler suite, a powerful development system. GNU gcc demonstrates its strength by allowing you to build the complete Linux system with it. In addition many programming languages and programming aids available on the internet can easily be used on a Linux computer. The list of compilable, scripting, or interpreted languages is long so we can list only a few samples here. Note there are usually various flavours of each language and often there are interpreted versions of the compilable languages available. Compilable: C, C++, Objective C, Fortran, Lisp, Pascal, Modula-2, Modula-3, Oberon, Scheme, Prolog, Ada, Apl, Eiffel, Forth,... Interpreted: Awk, Perl, Python, Tcl,...

  Complete software development platform

- Support of common standards means that Linux is to a great extent POSIX compatible and follows Unix traditions in almost every area. The benefits are the simple integration of Linux systems into existing Unix computer networks and the easy transfer of software to the Linux platform.

  Support of Unix standards

- The complete GNU software suite means all tools and programs from the GNU software project are available under Linux. Linux is therefore the de facto GNU operating system.[2]

  GNU software suite

Even if you can't follow some of the terms we are using at the moment, you will get a feeling for their meaning shortly and learn how best to draw on the benefits they imply.

---

[2] Initially the Free Software Foundation (FSF) planned for HURD to become the free GNU operating system. But after Linux integrated the complete GNU software within a very short time, HURD was no longer necessary and so, at least in practice Linux took the place of HURD.

1.1.2 Linux 2.0

Linux is well on its way to fame with the very comprehensive version 2.0.x release you have in your hands.

Next version

The big step from version numbers 1.2 to 2.0 is mainly due to the fact that Linux now supports not only its original development platform, the intel based PC, but also a large number of additional hardware plat-

New hardware platforms

forms. It is only a matter of time until complete, comprehensive, and stable systems like POWER LINUX will be available for other platforms.

In addition to the broad hardware support many drivers have been improved, and many new ones added. The network support has been

New drivers

completely worked over. This shows clearly in extended functioning and further improved performance. Figure 1.2 shows the new Linux logo which won the Linux 2.0 logo competition.

Fig. 1.2: The new Linux 2.0 logo.

The installation of Linux 2.0 offers new possibilities too. Kernel

Modularised kernel

modules (drivers which are loadable when the system runs) are supported in a logical manner, as well as a so-called "initial ramdisk". This makes required modules available after the start of the kernel and makes it possible to start the system directly after the installation without rebooting.

1.1.3 Standardization

Many efforts have already been made to transfer important standards

Standardisation

from the Unix world to Linux. Already there are Linux systems certified to the POSIX.1 standard. Some of the required changes are already integrated in the Linux 2.0 kernel, and one can expect that the kernel will fully support POSIX.1. The next step will be the XPG4 certification for Linux systems.

Caldera Inc. in Utah, USA is striving for Unix certification of Linux by 1997. Unix certification will definitely help Linux on the road to success. One will hear more on that subject in the near future within the frame of the "Caldera Open Linux" development.

Caldera Open Linux

There, in connection with internationalisation, National Language Support (NLS) will be added. The aim is to create a universal Linux system supporting the local customs of the user's own country. The scope of NLS ranges from formatting dates, time, and currencies in the local style, providing program text (e.g. menus and messages) in the appropriate language, and translating manual pages.

National Language Support

You may be familiar with the simplest of these problems if you have ever tried to adapt an English Linux version to German features (i.e. the extended character set and keyboard layout).

1.2 POWER LINUX

The POWER LINUX system before you is derived from the LST (Linux Support Team) distribution. LST is an independent German develop- ment, which has its roots at the University of Erlangen-Nuremberg. Some fundamental changes have been introduced with the creation of version 2.2 from LST:

Linux Support Team

- all software can be installed, removed, and updated using soft- ware management tools that work with the **rpm** package format;

Software package management

- complete conversion to ELF;[3]

- compatibility with Caldera and Red Hat Linux;

- orientation to the development of Caldera OpenLinux.

These reforms are due to an open and future-orientated develop- ment. It is true that certain habits have to be given up, but users will gain the possibility of using software components from the ever more popular Linux systems, Caldera OpenLinux and Red Hat Commercial Linux. For the most part these additional components can be used in the existing system without major conversions.

Easy integration of commercial components

If you want, for example, to use WordPerfect (Fig. 1.3) or Corel Draw for Linux, you will find these applications available in **rpm** pack- age format and for easy integration into your system.

Of course, POWER LINUX still supports the **tgz** package format used till now. It is still the main format used at the great Linux software archives such as sunsite.unc.edu and tsx-11.mit.edu.

tgz is still supported

---

[3] ELF - Executable and Linking Format

Fig. 1.3: Word Perfect for Linux.

LST
Software
GmbH

The development of LST is beeing continued by LST Software GmbH in Erlangen, Germany and POWER LINUX is based on Caldera OpenLinux Lite, the freely available version of Caldera OpenLinux.

1.2.1 LISA

In comparison to pioneering times, the installation of Linux systems has become much easier. Instead of getting a spartan input prompt (after a well meant "good luck!" message) and coping with further steps without manual or online help, one is now spoiled by convenient installation tools that simplify the decisions and knowledge of technical details formerly required of users.

Convenient
Linux
installations

These tools also help you avoid making serious mistakes during installation.

POWER LINUX offers you the LISA (Linux Installation & System Administration, Fig. 1.4) installation tool from LST, already familiar as the installation interface for the Caldera Network Desktop which is available worldwide.

LISA

LISA shouldn't present problems for users at any experience level. Nevertheless there is surely still enough material for this book, which will hopefully become a valuable companion for the installation and daily use of Linux. It should help you to find all the information you need allowing you to have as much fun in the daily use of Linux as we have had for years.

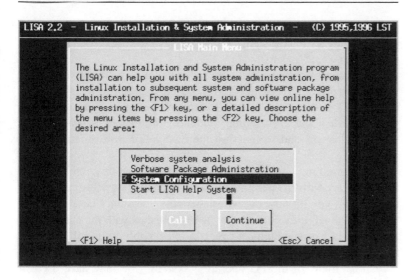

Fig. 1.4: The LISA main menu.

If you need additional literature on Linux that goes further than the *Initial aid* initial aid of this book, we especially recommend the following book:

Written by Dr. Fred Hantelmann it is titled "Linux Start-Up Guide" *Linux* and represents an excellent supplement to our own book. It too has been *Start-Up* published by Springer-Verlag and is part of the Linux Power Pack. The *Guide* ISBN is 3-540-62676-X.

1.3   General Information

Due to the quite different levels in readers' knowledge, it isn't easy for us to fulfil the expectations of every reader to the same extent. The *Different* already experienced PC or Linux user will be rather more interested in *knowledge* detailed hints for the Linux system, whereas a PC beginner will probably want to get more information about the fundamental processes of his or her computer.

If in doubt, we have decided to cover the facts in greater detail since *Comprehensive* beginners, in comparison to more advanced users already familiar with *information* the system, are much more dependent on comprehensive information about Linux. The experts will see, in any case, which sections they can pass over and the beginners will soon greatly appreciate the comprehensive information.

To work with Linux you must of course first install a Linux system. This normally proceeds without real problems, though some additional information is necessary in case there are initial difficulties.

We will explain what to do in such a case and basically what occurs when starting a Linux system so that you have the background to better understand what happens.

Planning help

If you successfully booted with the installation disk and your hardware was correctly recognized, you are on the way to installation of your own Linux system. We will provide assistance with organizing your hard disk space, planning your individual Linux system to best meet your needs, and completing the installation with minimal difficulty.

After installing your new Linux system, you can dive into an exciting adventure with an operating system which may have been relatively unknown to you till now but whose benefits you surely have heard of: "Unix". Though Linux cannot yet be embellished with the name Unix, it does in fact provide almost everything available in an official Unix release.

The legendary "Unix"

Unlike many of the PC operating systems you may have used in the past, Unix traditionally has been a multiuser system. Where previously you may have worked with such a system as a normal user, Linux now offers you the unique chance to gain practical experience as system administrator with unlimited access to the system. After all, it is your PC with which you can do whatever you want. Even if accumulated errors necessitate a new installation, on the whole you will have at least gained valuable experience.

Multiuser system

Imagine what would happen, if you, as system administrator, made a mistake within a Unix system used by many people every day. Initially, since you are probably the only user of your computer, a mistake will not affect anyone else. You can regard Linux as a big playground in which you collect valuable experience in the use and understanding of Unix and system administration.

Responsibilities of the system administrator

Of course, you can also use your Linux system as a serious production environment for software development, word processing, or as a private productive desktop. Figure 1.5 shows the launchpad, which supports your daily work with useful programs.

The versatility of Linux

Fig. 1.5: The launchpad of POWER LINUX .

In Chapter 5 we delve into details about the different programs and applications provided with the system and give you some ideas how to best use them.

The Basics

We assume that you bought a PC off the shelf with a pre-installed OS. Until today you were probably spared the task of installing a new operating system.

On the other hand, perhaps you have already gained a wealth of experience with various DOS, Windows, OS/2, and Linux installations. In this chapter we cover the essential steps for successful installation of the Linux operating system. Amongst the areas covered in this chapter are:

Installation basics

- operating systems

- the boot process

- the BIOS and its setup program

- hard disk partitioning and device names

- use of the **fdisk** program

- bootstrapping and system startup

2.1 Operating Systems

Before we explain how and why an operating system is loaded by your PC, we briefly discuss the function and peculiarities of operating systems in general.

Operating system

The most widely used operating systems for PCs today are OS/2 and MSDOS. Basic details of how these operating systems are set up and loaded are similar to Linux.

Once your computer has loaded an operating system it is ready to process your commands through a command line interpreter (CLI)[1] or a graphical user interface (GUI) (e.g. as with the Macintosh).

Command line interpreter

---

[1] For example this is **command.com** under DOS and **bash** under Linux.

Basic services

What distinguishes an operating system from a normal application program? In principle, the OS is software like every other application. It simply behaves a bit differently and serves one primary purpose: it provides all application programs with the basic functions that are required to fulfill their tasks.[2]

These basic functions handle, for example, the creation, opening, closing, and writting of files on external data storage devices, the management of the working memory, and control of all devices and cards in your computer.

You rarely notice these basic functions as they operate in the background. Normally your closest contact to the OS is the aforementioned command line interpreter. The command line interpreter in Unix is known as the shell.

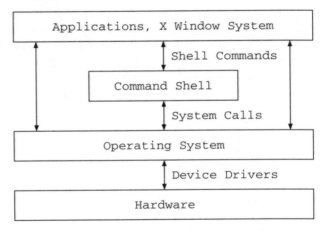

Fig. 2.1: Layer model of the Linux system architecture.

The interaction of the OS, computer, and the application software can be represented by a layer model (Fig. 2.1). In this diagram you can see that only the operating system, via its drivers, directly accesses the hardware. All other system components require the services of the OS to complete their tasks.

Operating system
characteristics

Normal applications program behaviour is to accept data in some form, manipulate it, and generate some output. The principal difference between an operating system and an applications program is that the applications program completes its assigned task and terminates;[3] an

---

[2] The operating system itself is not called upon directly. More often the application programs call the required functions from within the system libraries such as libc which in turn use the services of the operating system when needed.

[3] An exception is when the system "panics" and can no longer continue its normal function. In this case it displays the "kernel panic" message, attempts to save the current data and then terminates itself.

operating system does not reach an end condition. It is continuously
available to perform its services for the applications.

Naturally, an operating system can also be terminated or stopped. *shutdown*
This is usually referred to as a shutdown, and is effected by the
system administrator. Because of the multitude of unseen processes,
simply switching off the computer (as you may be used to doing) should
not be done.

When using DOS you simply switched off your computer when you
were finished. With Windows, you became used to closing applications
and leaving Windows before shutting off the computer. If you have been
using Windows 95 or NT, you are familiar with the use of a shutdown
process to be performed prior to powering down your computer.

With Linux it is essential that you properly shutdown the operating
system prior to switching off the power. Advanced operating systems
buffer, or keep in memory, some of the data that you have been working
with. If you fail to shut down properly, that data may be lost, files may
become corrupted, and other damage to your file system may occur.

In the following section we will discuss what happens when you
switch on the power to your computer, the boot process. You probably
take the reliability of your PC's boot process completely for granted.
However, when alterations to the system are undertaken and the computer may no longer boot correctly it becomes important to understand
more details of the boot process.

2.2 BIOS and Setup

When you switch on your computer the absolute minimum of program *The boot process –*
routines, the Basic Input Output System (BIOS), are located in the *all things have*
permanent Read Only Memory (ROM) and executed. *small beginnings*

With BIOS routines alone there is little useful interaction with your
computer. Your familiar applications and programs can only be started
after your computer has loaded the operating system. The first task of *BIOS*
the BIOS is to provide the mechanisms necessary to load an operating
system.

Thus we have already hinted at what is required in order to start an *Loading an*
operating system. First, it has to be loaded. After power-on the com- *operating system*
puter, with the help of its BIOS, determines where to find an operating
system (unless it finds a program or operating system in its memory).

In the case of the PC, the operating system data is usually found
on the floppy diskette drive or the first hard disk. [4] The computer will

---

[4] The latest BIOS variants partly support the booting directly from CDROM. This
is, for example, possible with the POWER LINUX CDROM.

Changing the boot drives on old computers

Installation without a floppy disk is also possible

Boot sequence

Protection from unauthorized access.

BIOS setup values

Dangerous setup tuning

normally first determine if there is a floppy disk in the boot drive. Recent computers always have a 3.5" drive as the boot drive.

However there are still many older computers with a 5.25" drive as their boot drive. These systems may even have an older BIOS which doesn't support swapping the boot drive assignment from the 5.25" unit to the 3.5" drive. Even in this case it is possible to boot from the 3.5" drive. If you have one of these older computers, we encourage you to do a bit of extra work: you should open your computer. There is normally a ribbon cable running from the motherboard of your computer to each of the two floppy disk drives. Simply reverse the order in which the cable attaches to your floppy drives. The boot drive is always the drive at the end of the floppy drive cable.

Now your computer too can boot from the 3.5" drive. But don't forget to register the change of the drives in the setup program of your computer as well.

If, however, you are concerned about taking screwdriver and cables in hand yourself, POWER LINUX offers the alternative of starting the installation directly from the CDROM via DOS. You will read more on this topic later.

If there is no disk in the boot floppy drive when starting, then the computer will try to get the data for an operating system from the hard disk. This order is not always maintained; newer computers often provide the ability to modify the order in which your compter checks drives for an operating system. This is done in the BIOS setup program where you can stipulate that the computer tries to boot from the diskette drive only after attempting to boot from the hard disk, or even simply ignore the diskette drives for boot purposes. This option is also interesting for increased security; many systems provide BIOS password protection that limits the ability of users to modify BIOS parameters.

If BIOS access has been password protected, users can only start installed operating systems. The computer cannot be manipulated from the outside via an "undesirable" boot diskette.

Returning to the setup program, we will now treat this topic in greater depth. The behaviour of the BIOS routines can be modified to a certain extent with the setup program. The setup program is part of the BIOS, and is available as soon as your computer is started.

With most computers you enter the setup by pressing a certain key or key combination immediately after power-on. If you have a new computer, the **delete** key will probably activate the setup sequence. Exactly how to enter the setup program of your computer should be obvious from the computer or motherboard manual, or may be indicated on the screen output whilst starting the PC.

Normally you will not need to change the BIOS setup. There are some users, however, who are fond of changing the settings to extract the utmost performance from their computer. Unfortunately, this "fine tuning" often produces problems for more efficient operating systems like Linux.

If unexplained errors appear during installation, (e.g. drivers behave erroneously, timing problems occur) don't hesitate to run the setup program and reset the BIOS to its default settings. This has helped some users to complete the Linux installation without further problems.

Recommendation: standard settings

Furthermore, the setup program often provides the opportunity to disable shadowing of the CMOS into the last 384 KB within the first megabyte of your computer's main memory, providing that 384 KB remains as free memory for the installation. This can be the decisive factor, allowing you to complete installation when your computer has very little main memory.

Shadowing

2.3 Booting

We now turn from the subject of the setup program and continue the discussion of booting an operating system. We already know that the computer searchs for the operating system data and then copies it into main memory. The operating system data can be located on various media. A single floppy diskette may serve this purpose, but normally it will be the hard disk.

A diskette usually offers just enough space for one operating system. So that it can be loaded by your computer the boot sector on the diskette must contain information about the type and size of this operating system. If this is the case, and this diskette is in the active boot drive at power-on, then the operating sytem on the diskette is loaded and started.

A diskette offers at most enough space for a single operating system

DOS will give you the input prompt (**A:>**) and some Linux systems may ask for further diskettes (the "root" or "ram" disks). In the case of POWER LINUX only a single diskette is required for starting the operating system.

Unlike a diskette, the hard disk offers the possibility of storing data for multiple operating systems. To allow selection between the various operating systems after power-on you need a boot manager.

Boot manager

With the exception of DOS almost every operating system is equipped with its own boot manager. For this purpose Linux has the LInux LOader (LILO) while OS/2 has the OS/2 Boot Manager. A boot manager can usually be configured to load other operating systems too. Note that there are commercial boot managers which may have advantages for some installations. These commercial products may simplify getting OSs such as Windows NT to coexist with Linux.

Apart from the fact that hard disks can be partitioned, the logical organization of hard disks and floppy diskettes is the same. The following explanation is therefore equally valid for both.

Booting

The whole process, up to the point when operating system data has been loaded into memory and the operating system started, is referred to as "booting". The following steps are required by Linux for this process.

- The master boot record (MBR) of the hard disk or the boot sector of the diskette is loaded.

- The first active partition is determined by checking the partition table in the MBR.[5]

- The primary boot loader, which is held in the MBR, now loads the boot sector of the active partition.

- The secondary boot loader in the active partition is started.

- The secondary boot loader gets the information from a map file[6] that maps the physical location of the system kernel on the diskette or hard disk and then loads that code into the main memory.

- The system kernel is started and takes over further control – the operating system runs.

Since we have already mentioned the term "partitioning" we should give a more detailed explanation of it.

2.4 Hard Disk Partitioning

Whilst a diskette, due to its small capacity, can provide only enough space for a single operating system, a hard disk can provide space for various operating systems on the same drive.

Partitioning – look before you leap!

To understand how these operating systems find their places on one single hard disk we must first understand how space on the drive is divided.

Every hard disk for PCs has a Master Boot Record (MBR), which contains information about the hard disk and the partition table as well. All important information about the size and structure of the hard disk and the division of its space, i.e. the partitioning, is contained in the MBR.

---

[5] This determination is, of course, not relevant for diskettes due to their lack of a partition table.
[6] The map file is a list of all sectors over which the system kernel is spread. While booting there is no file system structure available and so the system kernel can only be located with the help of the map file.

In the simplest case, your hard disk will contain only one partition that covers the entire area of the drive. In this case, though, it will be difficult to run various operating systems on it without modifying the partitioning of the hard disk.

Partitions

It is nevertheless possible to run multiple operating systems from a single partition. For example, OS/2 and DOS can coexist when they share the DOS file system structure. Using a slightly different technique, the "umsdos" exension for Linux allows a Linux file system to be created within a DOS file system.

Linux within a DOS partition

Though these solutions make life easier, for one need not worry about the partitioning of the hard disk, one pays for the higher convenience with a clear decrease in efficiency.

For this reason, and because of better structuring and data protection, the hard disk is most often divided into several areas, the partitions.

Within a partition an operating system can administer its own data and is protected from uncontrolled access by other operating systems. The partitions are independent data areas and can each contain their own file systems and operating systems.

Several partitions

How can we visualise this hard disk division? Hard disks as well as diskettes are physically divided into cylinders (in case of diskettes: tracks), heads, and sectors. A 1.44 MB diskette, for example, has 80 tracks, 18 sectors, and 2 heads. A typical 1 GB hard disk has 1024 cylinders, 32 sectors, and 64 heads.

Hard disk partitions are always set within cylinder bounds. In the example of a hard disk with 1 MB cylinders given above, the partition size would be some multiple of 1 MB. In Sect. 6.8, we will explore a more exact description of the physical division.

Partitions are set within cylinder bounds

From the logical point of view, diskettes and hard disks are accessed by sequentially numbered sectors. In this system the first logical sector equates to the first physical sector, that is sector 1, head 0, and cylinder or track 0.

Logical sector numbers

Since this sector can always be located, regardless of any BIOS limits or translations for the administration of large hard disks, it is most suitable for storing boot information. The computer can get this boot information and the partition table directly after power-on.

BIOS limits

The number of partitions located on one hard disk is registered in the MBR of that hard disk in the form of a partition table. Each partition's type, position, and size within the hard disk, and a marker indicating whether the partition is an active one is also registered there.

Partition table

There should be only one active primary partition on a hard disk and it is this partition which the BIOS selects to boot after power-on. [7]

Active partition

---

[7] OS/2's fdisk has no problems activating extended partitions.

15

There are two different types of partitions:

- primary partitions (1-4) (or 3 primary and 1 extended),

- logical partitions (5-16) (contained within an extended partition).

Four primary partitions at most

The partition table has space enough for at most four primary partitions. In case you want to divide the hard disk into more than four areas, you may designate one of the primary partitions as an extended partition. You may then designate logical partitions within that extended partition.

Figure 2.2 shows a partition table, which you display with the command **fdisk -l**.

```
                             xterm
root@lisa:~# fdisk -l

Disk /dev/hda: 64 heads, 63 sectors, 827 cylinders
Units = cylinders of 4032 * 512 bytes

    Device Boot  Begin  Start   End  Blocks   Id  System
/dev/hda1           1      1    254  512032+   6  DOS 16-bit >=32M
/dev/hda2      *   255    255    407  308448   83  Linux native
/dev/hda3         408    408    424   34272   82  Linux swap
/dev/hda4         425    425    827  812448    5  Extended
/dev/hda5         425    425    551  256000+  83  Linux native
/dev/hda6         552    552    678  256000+  83  Linux native
/dev/hda7         679    679    827  300352+  83  Linux native

root@lisa:~#
```

Fig. 2.2: A partition table

An active primary partition is necessary

Certain conditions must be met so that the computer boots a particular operating system. An operating system can only be booted (directly or indirectly) from a primary partition. At the same time it must be marked as active. [8]

Booting directly

Directly booting means that the boot loader (a boot manager which doesn't allow choosing between several operating systems, but which always loads a certain operating system) as well as the operating system is located on a primary partition.

Booting indirectly

Indirect booting means that a boot manager is located on a primary partition and makes it possible to load the operating system data from another, for example from an extended partition.

2.5 Device Naming

Distinguishing the partitions

With your hard disk divided into various partitions, and possibly more than one hard disk in your computer, the partitions must be clearly distinguishable by their respective names.

---

[8] In Fig. 2.2 recognizeable by "*" in the column "boot" after hda2.

DOS uses for this assignment the drive letters **C**, **D**, **E**, etc., which are not actually very meaningful. They neither clarify the position within the partition table nor the sequence of the partitions.

Drive letters

The drive letters **A:** and **B:** have a special status. They do not represent hard disk partitions, they refer instead to the first two diskette drives.

The drive letter **C:** is the most meaningful under DOS. It stands for the first primary partition on the first hard disk, in which there is a DOS file system.

All further letters are distributed according to a scheme that gives little information on the assignment of the drive letters to the respective partitions. The letter **D:** usually stands for the first logical partition within the extended partition of the first hard disk. [9]

Unclear scheme

If you add a second hard disk, the first primary partition on the second hard disk gets the letter **D:**. The first logical partition, which first got the letter **D:** is called **E:**, and all further partitions are also altered to the next letter. The logical partitions of the second hard disk are at the bottom of the league.

If, however, you add an IDE hard disk to a computer that previously had only SCSI hard disks, the drive letter **C:** will be shifted from the first primary partition of the SCSI hard disk to the first primary partition of the IDE hard disk.

Unwanted shift of the drive letters

You may have the impression that we are not happy about these drive letters and the way in which they are assigned (and then reassigned after you thought you had everthing working fine), so let's have a look at how Linux deals with this matter.

The partition labels under Linux are precise. The partitions are named by a fixed label, that gives exact information where and on which hard disk the respective partition is to be found. This is a good point to mention that under Linux all devices are treated as special files.

Precise labels under Linux

The partition labels, all as device files, consist of distinct parts:

- the prefix **/dev/**, as under Linux all device files are located in the directory **/dev**,

- a term for the device, like for example **fd** (floppy disk) for floppy drives, **hd** (hard disk) for IDE hard disks or **sd** (scsi disk) for SCSI hard disks,

- the device number, where the first device is either 0, the second 1 and so on or for hard disks the first device is **a**, the second **b** and so on,

- and as required, a further format specifier, such as **H1440** (high density, 1440 KB) for a 1.44 MB diskette drive.

[9] DOS does not allow two primary partitions to serve as DOS drives on the same hard disk.

Hard disk type

Sequence of the hard disks

Distinguishing the partitions

Extented partition

So, every partition label starts with the same prefix **/dev/**, which also applies for every other special device. Then the hard disk type **sd** for SCSI hard disks or **hd** for (E)IDE hard disks.[10]

The hard disks are consecutively numbered with the small letters **a**, **b**, **c**, ... The first hard disk gets the term **a**, the second gets **b**, etc. If you want to reach a certain hard disk partition, you must add the number of the desired partition, that is **1**, **2**, **3**, etc.

Therefore the first partition of the first hard disk in an (E)IDE system is named **hda1**. As the limitation of the BIOS of having at most four primary partitions pertains also to Linux, these partitions are named **hda1**, **hda2**, **hda3**, and **hda4**.

If one of these primary partitions is set as extended partition, the numbers from five up are used for each logical partition within the extended partition, e.g. **hda5** for the first logical partition.

Complicated? Not at all. For practice, here are some other examples:

- **/dev/hda2** stands for the second partition on the first IDE hard disk,

- **/dev/sda3** stands for the third partition on the first SCSI hard disk,

- **/dev/hdb** stands for the second IDE hard disk, [11]

- **/dev/sdc** stands for the third SCSI hard disk.

Hard disk is not the same as partition!

It is absolutely necessary to take into consideration the difference between a complete hard disk (**/dev/hda**) and a single partition of this hard disk (**/dev/hda1**). Entering the label of a complete hard disk on the command line only makes sense in one single case, namely when calling up **fdisk**, as it only operates on a whole hard disk. Otherwise you will always use the partition names only, like for example when formatting, mounting or booting.

Naming of diskette drives

The diskette drives also get a clear label. The labels of the diskette drives always start with **fd**, followed by the drive number and perhaps by further information about the capacity.

Contact with alien partitions possible

At a quick glance one might get the impression that the device names under Linux are more complicated than the drive letters under DOS or OS/2. By using the precise labels it is always clear, which partition or hard disk is meant. A further advantage is that with this system one clearly reaches the partitions of other operating systems too, which isn't possible at all under DOS.

---

[10] The XT hard disks, which are no longer common, are still supported. The term for the type is **xd**.

[11] For EIDE controllers: the first drive on the first cable is **hda** and the second on the cable is **hdb**. On the second cable the first drive is **hdc** and the second is **hdd**.

Thus one can not only reach another partition under Linux (such as a DOS partition on **hda1**), but also mount it for access within the Linux file system, without any problems. For most file systems you have not only read access, but also write access.

Inclusion of foreign partitions

Having organized a DOS partition under Linux, you will understand the advantages this brings. And if you install a second or third hard disk or remove the first, you will fully appreciate the descriptive labels under Linux.

During installation, note carefully which device names are to be utilized, as even the best safety checks of your installation program cannot prevent you from reformatting your valuable Linux archive partition, if you explicitly wish to. This problem, though, is not unique to Linux. Under DOS too, you should not confuse **format A:** with **format C:**.

Use the device names carefully!

2.6   The Use of fdisk

Now that we have reviewed the types and layout of partitions and the hard disk, it should be clear to you why we have explained these technical details. It is likely that you will need to make some alterations to the partition table of your hard disk. Linux is most at home in its own partition and so we would like to provide it with one.

Now we just need a suitable helper in order to experiment with the partitioning of the hard disk. This helper has the same name in most operating systems: **fdisk**. The **fdisk** program is always needed to display the layout of a partition table, to create new partitions or to delete existing partitions.

Woe betide ye, who playth with fire – fdisk

During the installation, **fdisk** is run directly from LISA if necessary. Later you can also start **fdisk** from the command line.

Out of the frying pan and into the fire

In Fig. 2.3 we have run **fdisk** as the system administrator, i.e. as root, and displayed the list of possible commands with the **m** command.

```
                              xterm
root@lisa:~# fdisk /dev/hda

Command (m for help): m
Command action
   a   toggle a bootable flag
   c   toggle the dos compatiblity flag
   d   delete a partition
   l   list known partition types
   m   print this menu
   n   add a new partition
   p   print the partition table
   q   quit without saving changes
   t   change a partition's system id
   u   change display/entry units
   v   verify the partition table
   w   write table to disk and exit
   x   extra functionality (experts only)

Command (m for help):
```

Fig. 2.3: The fdisk program.

Note that partitions created for a new operating system should be created with the **fdisk** which belongs to that operating system. That means you must create DOS partitions with the DOS **fdisk** and Linux partititions with the Linux **fdisk**. [12]

OS/2 Boot Manager

If you later want to use the OS/2 Boot Manager, you must use a small trick in order to slip a Linux partition past OS/2. First create the partition you intend to use as the Linux root partition with the OS/2 **fdisk** as a bootable OS/2 partition. Then during the Linux installation, change the type of this partition from OS/2 to Linux native and install as usual. The OS/2 Boot Manager doesn't notice the swindle and, while booting, allows selection of the Linux partition without complaining.

We will now examine the features of the Linux **fdisk** more closely. The help menu shown in Fig. 2.3 lists all the important commands.

Creating new partitions

In order to create new partitions enter the **n** (new partition) command. If there are still primary partitions, i.e. those numbered from 1 to 4, free you will be asked whether the new partition should be created as a primary partition or as a logical partition within an extended partition.

```
Command (m for help): n
Command action
l logical (5 or over)
p primary partition (1-4): p
```

If you decide to create a primary partition, then you must enter the partition number:

```
Partition number (1-4): 2
```

Now you have to enter the first cylinder for the partition on the hard disk. This must be one of the free cylinders offered:

```
First cylinder (255-827): 255
```

Partition size

The end of the partition can either be entered as a cylinder number or as the size that the partition should have. When you want to determine the partition end via the size, you can do this by prefixing the size by a **+** and appending an **M** for a size in megabytes or a **K** for a size in kilobytes. If you prefix the size with a **+** but do not append an **M** or **K**, **fdisk** will assume the size is in cylinders.

```
Last cylinder or +size or +sizeM or +sizeK ([255]-407): 407
```

---

[12] Admittedly, you don't always have to. Linux is very tolerant and is content with partitions created by foreign operating sytems. Nevertheless you should keep to this basic rule.

The newly created partition can now be marked as a Linux partition. This is achieved with the **t** (change partition's system ID) command. If you don't know the correct partition ID you can display a list of all known types with the **L** command.

System ID of a partition

```
Command (m for help): t
Partition number (1-7): 2
Hex code (type L to list codes): 83
```

Linux partitions have ID 83 and Linux swap partitions have ID 82. If you want to use a swap partition instead of a swap file for the swap space, then don't forget to create the swap partition while you are repartitioning!

Swap partition

If your partition table is already completely full,

```
Command (m for help): n
No free sectors available
```

you will first need to delete a partition with the **d** command. Consider the fact that after a partition is deleted all the files that were on it will be lost. Therefore, make a backup of the affected partitions and keep a boot diskette available, as well as the backup and restore programs on diskette. Usually you would re-create a smaller version of this partition and restore the previously backed up data into it.

Deleting a partition

It is also possible to move the data in an existing DOS partition to the beginning of the partition with the help of a hard disk optimizing program such as **speedisk** or **defrag** and then to trim down the partition with the **fips** program which can be found on the first CDROM in the directory **/tools**. The space made free in the partition table can then be used for Linux.

Shrinking a DOS partition

If you want to do this, then please be cautious about what you do and above all make a backup of your important files.

Don't forget the backup!

When you have finished altering the partition table, then you can either leave **fdisk** with the **w** command to write the changes back to the hard disk or use the **q** command to abandon the changes. As long as you do not use the **w** command your partition table will be unchanged.

Leaving fdisk

2.7 Bootstrapping

You know already how an operating system is loaded into the working memory. If the loading process is sucessful the operating system loads itself. As this happens you usually see a stream of messages on the screen. With DOS these are, for example, the output from device drivers (**config.sys**) or other programs which are automatically started (**autoexec.bat**).

Bootstrapping – pulling oneself up by the bootstraps

Kernel
initialisation

Linux or more precisely the Linux kernel displays its initialisation steps as it starts. These messages give you hints as to the reason for boot process problems if they should occur. Next we review the most significant initialisation messages and their meaning.

Messages from the
hard disk driver

The most important message is that from the hard disk driver. The driver should find all hard disks in your computer and report each with the correct data. Check at least once whether the number of cylinders, heads and tracks reported actaully match those given in the specification sheet of your hard disk (cf. 132).

Watch out for
deviant data

In most cases this will be correct, but should the reported data deviate there may be problems with the subsequent installation process. Therefore you should attempt to convince the driver that you have the correct data. How this is achieved is explained later.

Recognition of
CD-ROM drives

When your hard disk is correctly recognised the next step is the CD-ROM drive. In practice problems occur more frequently in this area than in any other. Either the driver doesn't yet support your brand new drive or it doesn't recognise the I/O address or interrupt correctly. You can also assist here.

Installation from
the hard disk

Even when this does not function there remains the possiblity of installing from a hard disk partition. In this case use an operating system which supports your CD-ROM drive, copy the required files (only the minimun when space is short) locally to a hard disk partition and make them available, e.g. via the network with NFS, for your computer. Exactly which parts of the installation data you need to copy can be found on page 40.

Specify a hard disk
partition instead of
a CD-ROM drive

During the installation, specify the hard disk partition where you copied the data to as installation source instead of the unsupported CD-ROM drive. Also be sure not to specify that partition as one to be included in the present installation. Be aware, that it has to be a linux partition from which you provide the installation data.

2.8   The System Start

Your first Linux system startup occurs more quickly than you would think. It is already active when you have booted with the installation diskette and supports the installation process.

A special
installation
system

This special Linux system, which we have accommodated on a single diskette, provides you with all the utilities necessary to successfully install the final system. Your installation effort is aided by LISA, the Linux Installation and System Administration tool from LST.

A further feature of POWER LINUX is that you can use your new Linux system immediately after installation without having to reboot the PC.

2.8.1 The Generic Linux Kernel

A significant advance in Linux 2.0.x is the ability to run the system with a generic kernel. The kernel is, so to speak, the heart of the system. It provides the interface between the rest of operating system and the hardware. *Generic kernel – small is beautiful*

The operating system allows the application programs access to the hardware resources of the system such as memory, the hard disk, and perhaps a CD-ROM drive. Each of these resources, referred to as devices, is controlled by a device driver. *Management of system ressources*

These drivers allow for correct and exclusive access to the device. The operating system alone decides how and when a driver comes into action. This ensures, for example, that not more than one program may write to the same area of the hard disk at the same time.

The kernel, put very simply, represents a collection of various drivers, which are required in order to manage all the hardware in your computer. *Drivers*

In Linux 1.2.x it was still common that most drivers were held directly in the kernel. It was, nevertheless, possible to separate certain drivers from the kernel and to load them as kernel modules into the kernel on demand. *Loadable drivers*

The advantage of this method is that the kernel must not contain all conceivable drivers at once. Support for various hardware is obtained from the corresponding kernel module. This is particularly important for installation, which should support the most diverse computer configurations.

Each driver held directly in the kernel represents a potential source of conflicts, in that it may affect or disrupt hardware during its initialization. *Fewer conflicts*

Through the relocation of drivers into individual kernel modules hardware conflicts during the boot process may be significantly reduced.

Due to a logically conducted modularization and other improvements in Linux 2.0.x even the hard disk support is first installed at runtime. The remaining generic kernel holds only the drivers for the memory, screen and keyboard. *Kernel modularisation*

Such a minimal kernel may also be started on different hardware without conflicts. The long running and well known boot process problems of installation are largely a thing of the past.

Of course even loadable kernel modules are no cure all for hardware problems. When a particular hardware controller is not set for the default values expected by the loadable module, then the module must also be given the correct values. The technical details, for example the exact syntax for giving parameters to the kernel module, are taken over as far as possible by LISA. *Loadable module parameters*

Autoprobing

*Kernel module
parameters*

Tailor made kernel

Autoprobing allows a driver to search various memory locations for devices. Unfortunately some kernel modules are not capable of auto-probing. In practice, conflicts were often caused by autoprobing while attempts were made to recognize hardware.

Due to the absence of autoprobing, port addresses and interupts for these devices must now be given more frequently as parameters. This shouldn't really be a problem if you have your hardware documents within reach.

When you finally have your new system ready and in operation you can decide whether you want to continue to use the generic kernel from the installation diskette and leave it to the system to load the required drivers as kernel modules, or whether you configure a special kernel which holds the right drivers for your hardware.

It's about time now for some action. Following the general theory explained in this chapter we next explain the installation process in detail. This will enable you to understand all the significant steps.

Installation

After all this theoretical preparation we now finally come to the practical part. If you do not want to do the installation from the CD-ROM via a DOS system, with the help of the **install.bat** program, then you will need an installation diskette.

install.bat

3.1   The Installation Diskette

The batch file **install.bat** calls the program **loadlin.exe** which begins the installation just as if you had booted with the installation diskette. If, however, TSR programs or the use of memory managers cause problems with **loadlin.exe**, you should resort to the installation diskette.

loadlin.exe

If you have invested in the new LINUX POWER PACK and there is already a installation diskette enclosed, then just use that.

If there is no ready made installation diskette with your POWER LINUX , you will need to transfer it from the CD-ROM. For this purpose there is a small batch program **bootdisk.bat** in the top directory of the CD-ROM which will create the installation diskette for you under DOS or OS/2.

Creating an installation diskette

To create a boot diskette whilst using a Unix system it is best to use the **dd** program. Insert a formatted diskette into the diskette drive, change to the **\1st_22\bootdisk** directory on the CD-ROM and enter the following command:

Using dd

```
dd if=bootdisk.raw of=/dev/fd0 bs=18k
```

As well as the installation diskette you may also require a second diskette, the module diskette which holds drivers for special hardware.

Additional drivers are on the modules diskette

The installation diskette from POWER LINUX contains, as previously described, a generic kernel, and a complete Linux installation system. The installation system is in an "initial ramdisk" that is uncompressed and started for the installation process just after the kernel is loaded.

25

Assuming your **BIOS** has been set up to support booting from the floppy drive, insert the installation diskette in the boot drive and switch on the computer.

3.2 Booting for Installation

LILO

The Linux boot loader LILO now starts and you see the first POWER LINUX display. It gives a short message about available boot labels and some few parameters for the generic kernel.

Keyboard layout

At the point at which you see the LILO boot menu, it is unfortunately not possible to support non-US keyboard layouts. For the most part the US keyboard layout, which is the default when your computer is switched on, differs from your national keyboard layout only in the position of special characters.

Important special characters

For the boot parameters the most important special characters are the "**=**" and the "**/**".

To get an idea where to find the needed characters on a non-US keyboard we show you as an example the translation table for a German keyboard.

Character	[z]	[y]	[/]	[=]	[-]	[_]
Key	[y]	[z]	[-]	[']	[ß]	[?]

Boot parameters – how do I explain it to my kernel?

Boot parameters are a way to inform the kernel about particular hardware settings when it doesn't recognise them by itself. In the same way particular drivers can be deactivated by the use of boot parameters. As the generic kernel now contains very few drivers it will probably not require any boot parameters.

IDE drivers

The generic kernel only supports IDE hard disks and ATAPI CD-ROM drives linked to the IDE controller. Thus there is only one boot parameter which is important for the IDE driver if all your hardware hasn't been clearly recognized:

hdx=cdrom or **hdx=cyls,heads,sects**.

Assign ports

In the first case, you have to signal the driver that there is a CD-ROM drive on an IDE port. In the following table you can see exactly which parameter you need:

CD-ROM often connected to the second IDE Port

CD-ROM as master on the first IDE port	**hda=cdrom**
CD-ROM as slave on the first IDE port	**hdb=cdrom**
CD-ROM as master on the second IDE port	**hdc=cdrom**
CD-ROM as slave on the second IDE port	**hdd=cdrom**

In case you don't know how your CD-ROM drive is connected, first try **hdc=cdrom**, as there is often an IDE drive connected as master to the first IDE port, and the ATAPI CD-ROM is connected to the second IDE port, also as master.

If your hard disk hasn't been recognized correctly, then you need to use the second variant of the **hdx=** boot parameter. Use the following as an example, but insert the right parameters for your hard disk:

Parameter for the hard disk

```
hda=827,64,63
```

For cases in which an IDE port should not be initialized at all, e.g. you have brand new hardware connected to the port, which the driver doesn't know of or treats incorrectly, then use the following statement:

Disableing an IDE port

```
hdx=noprobe
```

You can also state several parameters at the same time, for example:

```
hda=827,64,63 hdb=cdrom hdc=noprobe hdd=noprobe
```

You need to use these boot parameters only when the kernel cannot recognize your hard disk or CD-ROM drive by itself. Try loading the kernel without additional parameters first. Press the **TAB** key to get an overview of the kernel labels available for selection. For the the installation you need only the kernel labelled **install**. As this is the default kernel it suffices to simply press **RETURN**.

Parameter usually not necessary

The kernel holds a limited number of device drivers that are initialized in sequence and produce various messages. Take your time to digest all these messages and attempt to extract useful information from them.

Output from the kernel during initialization

Should a read error occur whilst loading from the diskette, you will have to create a new installation diskette from the CD-ROM. Be sure to use a brand name diskette, preferably new.

Only use top quality diskettes

Above all it is important that every IDE hard disk is correctly recognized for the installation. The manufactuer, size, as well as the number of cylinders, heads, and sectors should be reported. Correct information about the use of partitions should also be given.

Check for correct recognition of hard disks

The generic kernel only holds drivers for (E)IDE hard disks and ATAPI CD-ROM drives connected to the IDE controller. All other drivers are loaded with the help of the kernel module manager.

The output of a kernel module that is loaded later is usually the same as that during the kernel initialization and is displayed by the installation program on a seperate console. You will read more about this later.

Output of a kernel module corresponds to that of the kernel driver

Studying the driver messages should give a feeling for how to interpret the kernel output. We have clarified the way these messages are displayed so that they are easier to review.

Shifting drivers into kernel modules

Improvement of clarity was also the reason for relocating all possible modules external to the kernel. Since they are then loaded only on demand, the number of kernel messages during booting is reduced and the remaining messages are easier to survey and understand.

3.2.1　Linux Kernel Boot Messages

Example boot process

At this point let us explain in greater detail the output from the various drivers using an example boot procedure.[1] The following presents the kernel output as it initialises. This should make it easier for you to check that your hardware is being identified and initialised correctly.

As soon as LILO has begun to load the kernel you will be able to see the progress of the loading process in the form of periods displayed on the console:

```
Loading install........................
```

Once the compressed Linux kernel has been loaded from the diskette into main memory, it is decompressed. You will recognise this by the message:

```
Uncompressing Linux ... done
```

Following this the kernel is started:

```
Now booting the kernel
```

And then it sequentially checks for the hardware in the computer according to which drivers are in the kernel.

The kernels drivers emit messages as they are initialized

Each driver gives out more or less detailed messages from which one can draw conclusions about the hardware present and its initialization. The course of the boot procedure (depending naturally on the hardware and kernel used) may appear as follows:

Initializing the screen:
```
>>> kernel: initializing video console <<<
Console: 16 point font, 400 scans
Console: colour VGA+ 80x25, 1 virtual console (max 63)
```

Initializing the BIOS:
```
>>> kernel: initializing PCI devices <<<
pcibios_init : BIOS32 Service Directory structure at
0x000fb800
pcibios_init : BIOS32 Service Directory entry at 0xfbc10
pcibios_init : PCI BIOS revision 2.00 entry at 0xfbc40
Probing PCI hardware.
```

---

[1] The output will naturally vary from computer to computer.

Calculating the computers relative speed:

```
>>> kernel: calculating speed index <<<
Calibrating delay loop.. ok - 19.97 BogoMIPS
```

Initializing main memory:

```
>>> kernel: initializing memory <<<
Memory: 14980k/16384k available (824k kernel code, 384k
reserved, 596k data)
This processor honours the WP bit even when in supervisor
mode. Good.
```

Initializing network support:

```
>>> kernel: initializing networking devices <<<
Swansea University Computer Society NET3.035 for Linux 2.0
NET3: Unix domain sockets 0.12 for Linux NET3.035.
Swansea University Computer Society TCP/IP for NET3.034
IP Protocols: IGMP, ICMP, UDP, TCP
Swansea University Computer Society IPX 0.34 for NET3.035
IPX Portions Copyright (c) 1995 Caldera, Inc.
```

Checking processor characteristics:

```
>>> kernel: check CPU <<<
Checking 386/387 coupling... Ok, fpu using exception 16
error reporting.
Checking 'hlt' instruction... Ok.
```

Showing the kernel version:

```
>>> kernel: show kernel version <<<
Linux version 2.0.7 (root@lisa.1st.de) (gcc version 2.7.2)
#1 Sun Jul 14 13:24:26 MET DST 1996
```

Initializing the serial and parallel ports:

```
>>> kernel: initializing character devices <<<
Serial driver version 4.13 with no serial options enabled
tty00 at 0x03f8 (irq = 4) is a 16550A
tty01 at 0x02f8 (irq = 3) is a 16550A
lp1 at 0x0378, (polling)
```

Initializing the (E)IDE controllers (in this case with an ATAPI CD-ROM):

```
>>> kernel: initializing block devices <<<
hda: QUANTUM FIREBALL1280A, 1222MB w/83kB Cache, LBA,
CHS=621/64/63
hdc: FX400D, ATAPI CDROM drive
ide0 at 0x1f0-0x1f7,0x3f6 on irq 14
ide1 at 0x170-0x177,0x376 on irq 15
```

Initializing the diskette controller and the diskette drive:

```
Floppy drive(s): fd0 is 1.44M, fd1 is 1.2M
FDC 0 is a post-1991 82077
```

Testing the partition table:

```
>>> kernel: check disk partition tables <<<
Partition check:
hda: hda1 hda2 hda3 hda4 < hda5 >
```

Apparent kernel
error messages

Along with the correct kernel output produced by the initialisation of hardware, the generic Linux kernel from the installation diskette may also give apparent error messages.

This is always the case when a kernel driver does not find the hardware that it seeks, because it simply is not in your computer.

That drivers for hardware not present in the computer generate error messages saying that the hardware they sought could not be found is perfectly OK.

These messages are harmless and need not cause you further concern. The kernel tells you what hardware is currently sought and whether it is recognised. If, for example, the following message appears:

pci_init: no BIOS32 detected

it merely means that the computers BIOS does not support the PCI bus. You should ensure that your installed hardware is correctly recognised by the drivers.

In comparison to the Linux variants known to date, the installation of POWER LINUX using its generic kernel has become significantly

Shifting drivers
into kernel modules

clearer, because alongside the absolutely necessary drivers (e.g. memory, screen, keyboard) it contains only support for (E)IDE hard disks and ATAPI CD-ROM drives.

Many of the confusing messages from non-relevant CD-ROM and network drivers are therefore eliminated completely. The patches for POWER LINUX are highlighted with (>>> ... <<<) for clarity.

3.3 Dealing with LISA

Having become acquainted with the boot process, we can now go on to the much more pleasant part. As soon as the Linux kernel is booted and started successfully, LISA goes into action.

LISA is
easy to use

Dealing with LISA shouldn't be a problem for you. But it will do no harm to give some explanation on how to best utilize this program.

Every LISA menu is treated in the same way. You can call up the online help for each menu (Fig. 3.1) with the **F1** key.

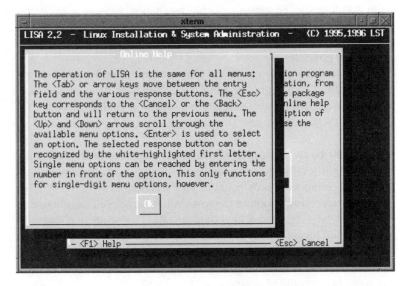

Fig. 3.1: LISA's help menu

You can move between the individual menu options and the response buttons with the **TAB** key.

TAB leaps to the next button

With the **Up** and **Down** cursor keys you choose between the individual menu options, and the **Left** and **Right** cursor keys can also be used for selecting a response button.

If not all menu items can be shown within a scroll window this is indicated by an arrow at the edges above and below the scrollbar. The arrow points out that there are still other menu options, which are not currently visible.

Scroll bar

Each menu item is numbered so that you can directly choose items 0 to 9. Menu items over 9 cannot be selected this way but must be selected with the **up** and **down** cursor keys. You can also skip back and forth a whole menu page with the **Page Up** and **Page Down** keys.

Choose the menu displays directly

If a menu item cannot be displayed in full (e.g. more comprehensive software package descriptions), this is indicated by an ellipsis (**. . .**) at the end of the menu entry. You can see the complete text of these menu entries in a special window with the **F2** key.

Display lines in full length with F2

Depending on the menu in question you can choose an entry or confirm an answer with the **OK** button. With the **ESC** key, as well as with the **Cancel** button, you can skip back to the last menu or leave LISA.

3.4 The Kernel Module Manager

The installation
process is subject
to changes

After LISA has taken control of the installation process it may vary from one POWER LINUX version to the next. This is because LISA continually tries to optimize the installation by simplifying the process as much as possible.

Always try to
get the latest
installation diskette

As in so many other cases, the POWER LINUX software is always one step ahead of its corresponding documentation. It is enough then to have received a newer installation diskette or update diskettes for POWER LINUX to have new functions or improved processes at your disposal.

So don't be too frustrated if the actual sequence of the following steps is slightly different from that described in the documentation. In every case changes are only made to your advantage.

Language and
keyboard layout

After successfully booting the installation kernel you can choose an installation language and a keyboard layout. The respective language and keyboard layout are then loaded from the installation diskette.

Note that you cannot modify them again during this installation and that both are transferred to the new system. There, of course, most settings can be modified again.

Overview
of already
recognized
devices

Next LISA signals whether any hard disk or CD-ROM drives have been recognized already. If this is the case and you need no further hardware support for the installation and running the system afterwards, then you don't have to worry about the kernel module administration during installation.

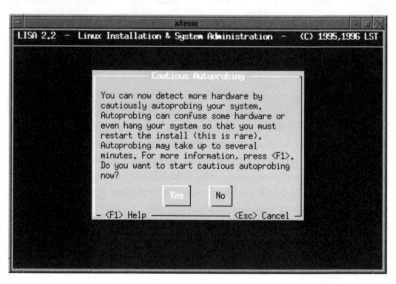

Fig. 3.2: Start autoprobing for further hardware?

This will be the case when you are using only an (E)IDE hard disk and an ATAPI CD-ROM drive for the installation.

If further hardware support is required to access the installation source or the destination partitions, the Linux system then asks you if you want to start autoprobing, i.e. the automatic detection of further hardware components (Fig. 3.2). Usually, after running autoprobing all needed hardware support will show up and you can continue with the installation.

Autoprobing for detection of further hardware

In a few cases, however, it could happen, that your computer hangs while autoprobing for further hardware. In this case, or if autoprobing doesn't show up the needed hardware components, you have the opportunity to call up the kernel module administration from the following menu.

Entering the kernel module manager

Each time you successfully load a new kernel module you will return to the first hardware information menu (Fig. 3.3). Here you will find out if the hardware has been recognized, and continue to load additional driver modules as necessary.

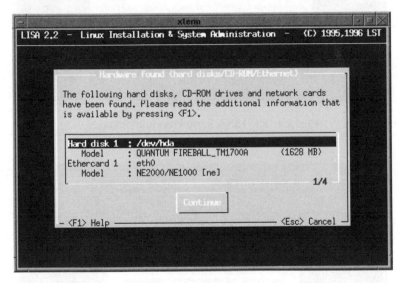

Fig. 3.3: Hardware already been detected by LISA.

The module manager of LISA makes it possible to load additional drivers, which are not included in the standard kernel, whenever required (Fig. 3.4).

Since the boot kernel only contains drivers for (E)IDE hard disks and ATAPI CD-ROM drives, which are run by the IDE controller, you must first load those drivers which are necessary for other hardware. To support this the following items are provided in the 'load kernel module' section of the module manager (Fig. 3.5):

Late loading the necessary modules

- CD-ROM drives

- SCSI controller

- Network cards

- PCMCIA cards

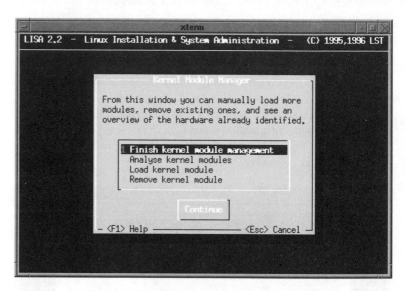

Fig. 3.4: The LISA kernel module manager.

Fig. 3.5: Loading kernel modules with LISA.

Select the areas which contain the additional modules necessary for the installation.

The installation diskette only contains kernel modules for common hardware, for example all Adaptec SCSI controllers and NE2000 or 3COM 3C509 network cards.

In case a module necessary for your hardware isn't amongst the kernel modules offered, you must choose the item "Load further modules from diskette", and have the module diskette ready, because it will now be required. After the necessary modules have been loaded from it you can select from them, too.

The module diskette contains further drivers

You can specify additional parameters to give the module a different IO port or interrupt if you don't succeed in initializing a kernel module with the default values.

Parameters for kernel modules too

You will receive a message if the initialization of a module has been successful, and you can continue loading further modules until all kernel modules necessary for the installation have been installed.

3.5 Setting Swap Space

As soon as you leave the kernel module manager you have the opportunity to make additional virtual memory available for the installation. This is called "swap space", as it refers to a special area ("space") on your hard disk, to which the system can transfer ("swap") unused parts of the main memory, when required. In principle this hard disk space is used as a direct addition to the existing main memory.

Swap space

So if you make available additional swap space, you actually extend your memory. Though swapspace in principle seems to be equivalent to the main memory under Linux, there is nevertheless a significant difference. In comparison to the main memory the access time to the swap space is significantly longer, resulting in noticeable waiting periods whenever your system draws on this additional memory.

Free memory upgrade

Loss in speed

You will especially notice this if you want to run the X Window system with less than 8 MB main memory. So much swapping may occur in this limited memory space that the use of numerous applications simultaneously will bring the computer almost to a standstill.

So swap space is no remedy for memory shortage but it makes it possible for the system to draw on this reserve in the short term, in situations in which more memory is needed than is actually physically there.

Reserves for the short term

There are two different ways to set swap space:

- as a swap partition on a partition which is specially created for it,

- as a swap file within an existing Linux partition.

35

Swap file blocks the
partition for the
installation

Both methods have advantages and disadvantages. If you already have a Linux partition at your disposal, you can set and activate a swap file on this partition. But note that you can no longer use this partition for your new Linux file system during the installation, as the partition needs to be formatted for this purpose. This isn't possible, though, as long as a swap file is located there. Otherwise you can, of course, set aside a seperate swap partition.

Faster access to
swap partition

Access to a swap partition is significantly faster than to a swap file, especially when the swap partition is located on a hard disk other than the one containing the root file system. The size of a partition, though, can only be changed with **fdisk**, which is relatively complicated, whereas the size of a swap file can be changed at any time without problem.

Recommendation
for swap space size

If you have only 8 MB main memory we recommend you create at least a 16 MB swap space. Having 16 MB main memory or more the optimum size depends on the intended purpose of your Linux system. A common guideline is to reserve a swap space at least equal to or slightly larger than your main memory.

Graphical
applications
need a lot of
memory space

If you want to use your X Window system intensively and to compile very often or use graphical applications, we recommend you use at least a 16 MB, or better 32 MB swapspace. A rule of thumb is to not make savings in swapspace when you have a lot of hard disk space at your disposal.

Start of the
installation
systems

After setting the swapspace the installation system in the initial ramdisk is started. This is evident by the fact that a number of virtual consoles are immediately available. This means you can log in as user "hilfe" or "help" on another console to start the POWER LINUX installation help system.

3.6   Automatic Hardware Analysis

Automatic
system
analysis

As all necessary hardware for the installation should be initialized now, LISA executes the system analysis to check. The system analysis establishes what hardware is in your computer, determines which drivers are used, and states important settings of your system. In Fig. 3.6 you can see the hardware information established by LISA.

Basis for further
installation

The values established are the basis for further installation and are used as references. If they are correct you should, for the most part, only have to confirm the settings suggested.

Changes are only
necessary for
incorrect values

Only change the values given by LISA when they are wrong or incomplete. Compare the outputs with the existing hardware in order to discover differences and problems. You can also see from the messages which hardware has been recognized and how it has been initialized.

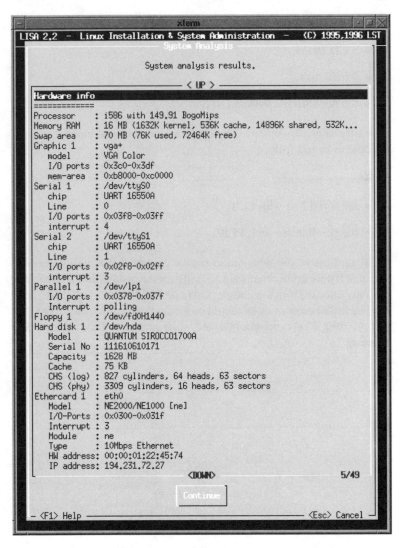

Fig. 3.6: The results of the LISA hardware analysis

3.7 The Installation Source

In order to be able to install the Linux system, LISA has to know where
to find the utility programs and the POWER LINUX series with the individual software packages. You must designate which of the offered
sources is appropriate.

*Necessary data for
the installation*

37

Various media can be used as the installation source:

- a CD-ROM,

- a hard disk,

- the network file system (NFS).

Furthermore, if supported by the LISA version you have, it may be possible to install from:

- a tape streamer,

- the serial line with SLIP,

- the parallel line with PLIP.

Existing components Regardless of the installation source chosen, LISA will determine which software components are actually on the installation source. You can only choose from the components that LISA finds.

The installation sources should be located in the directory **/1st_22** and in turn it should contain the subdirectories **bin**, **data** and **install**.

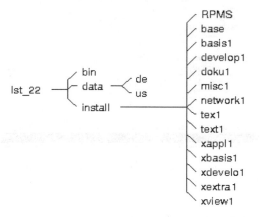

Fig. 3.7: The directory structure of the installation data

In the **bin** directory there should be the programs **cpio**, **rpm** and **rpmextr**. The directory **data** contains the index tables and database files and, finally, the directory **install** contains the real installation data.

Note that there is a difference between the directory slash **/** under Linux and the backslash **** under DOS and OS/2. In case the installation data are located on another place, the installation program will ask for the correct path.

3.7.1 Installation from CD-ROM

POWER LINUX offers you the selection of various CD-ROM drives that are supported by the Linux kernel. If your drive has already been recognized correctly the selection field should automatically be located over the correct CD-ROM drive.

If your CD-ROM drive hasn't been recognized already, or it is not on the list, you may have forgotten to load the respective kernel module with the kernel module manager.

Experts also have the chance to specify a drive name under the last item, "others". This also requires initialisation of the respective driver for the specified device.

When your drive is amongst the list of supported drives the installation program tries to mount it, or if there is no driver for the drive already, to first load the driver as a kernel module.

If you don't succeed in loading the kernel module, then, just as in the kernel module manager, there is still the option of giving the module additional parameters.

The parameters for a driver as kernel module are sometimes different from the parameters for the driver when it is integrated in the Linux kernel. LISA assists you by taking over the "translation" and allows you to set the same boot parameter for a loadable kernel module as for the boot process of the kernel.

If the CD-ROM can be mounted, the next step is to check if you have access to the POWER LINUX installation data on the CD-ROM. If this isn't possible or the CD-ROM is not an original LST 2.2 version, [2] you will probably have to get there by a rather roundabout way using a hard disk partition, as described below.

---

[2] LISA checks with a copy protection mechanisim whether or not the CD-ROM mounted is an original POWER LINUX installation CD-ROM. If an error is reported on this, ensure that you haven't inserted the "software" CD-ROM instead of the "installation" CD-ROM.

3.7.2 Installation from the Hard Disk

You will most probably install from the hard disk only if you don't succeed in installing directly from CD-ROM, or if there is no CD-ROM drive directly connected to the computer itself.

Shifting the installation data

For this way, you need to have already a running Linux system on your computer. Just copy the content of the **1st_22** directory from the CD-ROM to a sufficiently large Linux partition, e.g. via a local network with NFS.

LISA will then have access to the installation data from this partition. Of course you do not have to copy all the installation data.

Not every file has to be copied

It's enough to copy the basic system (Series **basis1**) and maybe the development and documentation components (Series **develop1** and **doku1**) to be able to install a basic system that runs.

The other components can later be installed step by step. Once you have a running system, you can compile a kernel for your system with which you can operate the CD-ROM drive. You can then install other software packages from the CD-ROM with a lot less effort.

Attention! Do not copy RPMS!

You must not copy the directory **RPMS** in the directory **install**, as it contains only hardlinks to the rpm files which are contained in the series directory **install**.

3.7.3 Installation over the Network (NFS)

NFS installation requires network experience

If you want to install per NFS (i.e. via the network) you should already have had some experience with networks and must be able to provide details of the IP address, network mask, and broadcast address to install from an NFS server for your computer.

IP addresses must be set

Furthermore, the IP address of the router and the NFS server are also requested, as well as the directory in which the POWER LINUX installation data is held. This directory can then be mounted.

LISA allows you to specify any path at all to the installation data. This can also consist of two independent parts in case you can mount an NFS directory under an alias but not under the whole pathname.

3.8 Specifying the Target Partition

Test system

When choosing a suitable target partition you must decide whether you want to provide Linux with its own partition or start out with a "test system" located within an existing DOS partition.

Installation within a DOS partition is to be recommended especially if you don't want to change the partitioning of your hard disk yet.

For this convenience one has to pay with a clear loss of performance, for in this case there is still a slow and, regarding the possibilities, limited DOS filesystem beneath the Linux extended-2 file system. All features of the extended-2 filesystem have to be emulated and this results in the performance loss.

*Loss in perfor-
mance under
umsdos*

Linux is only able to demonstrate its true qualities when it exists in its own native partition. If you want to work more intensively with Linux in the long run, you should provide a native partition for the system.

*A native partition
is optimal*

LISA offers all available Linux and DOS partitions for selection of the target partition. If you haven't yet created any Linux partitions, or you want to change the existing partitions, you can do it now with the **fdisk** program. Select that option from the menu.

*Setting new
partitions
with fdisk*

We have already described the use of the **fdisk** program on page 19. In the POWER LINUX help system you will also get further information on the use of **fdisk**.

If, with great foresight, you already left space enough for a further partition on your hard disk, it will be especially easy for you now.

Normally, though, your hard disk will be completely populated by partitions in use. In this case you must reduce or delete an existing partition in order to create space for a new Linux partition. Once you have made space then just leave it open (unformatted and unallocated). It will be applied and used as a Linux partition by the installation program.

*Repartitioning
can be necessary*

Note that the division of an existing partition into two partitions results in the loss of all the data in this partition! Although there are tools like **fips**, with which partitions can be reduced, we recommend their use only when you are more acquainted with hard disk partitioning.

*Attention:
loss of data!*

You should, therefore, first make a backup of these partitions. After the reduced partition has been re-created for the old operating system you can restore the saved data, well, at least the part for which there is still enough space.

*Backup
important
data*

If you prepared one or more partitions for Linux with the help of **fdisk** a reboot is performed for the purpose of making the changed partition settings valid. After the reboot, proceed in the same manner as you did during the first boot process and choose a newly defined Linux partition as the target partition for the installation.

*Changes
are only valid
after a reboot*

This partition will be first formatted and then mounted as the future root partition. The root partition contains the highest directory (the "root") of your data system. Note that the formatting of a partition is irrevocable. Therefore you should carefully note which partition you are formatting (see Chap. 2.5)!

Once the future root partition has been mounted you also have the chance of formatting other Linux partitions and integrating them to the new root filesystem. Normally you would install the complete system on one single partition.

*Integrating
further
partitions*

41

After integrating each desired partition the preparation stages are finished and you can continue on to choose the software components.

If you don't want to install your complete Linux system on one single partition, but would rather distribute it across several different partitions, you can specify the directory in which the additional partitions are to be integrated within your future system.

Setting /usr or /home to a special partition

The **/usr** and **/home** directories, for example, are just asking to be set on special partitions. Then you can administer certain areas, like the user data or home directories, independently from the root filesystem. For example, during a system upgrade you could change the root partition independently.

During installation, the future root partition (that is, the root of the whole data system) is mounted under the directory **/**. Each additional partition integrated will then be mounted within this future root filesystem. This has the result that each file lying at the end of a path which runs onto an extra partition that you have mounted, does not land up on the current root partition, but rather on that extra partition.

Additionally we can also recommend that you create an "archive partition" for your private work and data.

In case you have to make a complete new installation (because, for example, you have just received a great new Linux version), you will have the problem of how best to retain your important data.

An archive partition makes new installations easier

If you made copies of all important data on a special archive partition, which you integrated for example at **/archive** in the filesystem, you can feel free to delete the old root partition in preparation for the new installation. The archive data are secure on the separate partition and are therefore not affected by the new installation.

If in doubt, a single root partition is adequate

But if you have no idea yet how best to divide your filesystem (if at all), it will do no harm to just choose a single large root partition.

3.9 Choosing the System Software

There are three different ways of choosing the software for your Linux system:

- predetermined selection (minimal, standard or maximum system),
- compact selection by areas of application,
- individual selection by software series or single packages

Quick selection

The predetermined selection makes every decision for you and just pre-selects a minimal, recommended, or maximum system.

Selection by applications

The compact selection makes it possible to easily and quickly assemble a system for various application areas.

The individual or series selection requires more time but gives you the utmost freedom to decide upon the details.

Which selection method you should choose will depend on your knowledge and needs. If you are not acquainted with the Linux software packages and if you don't make great demands on your system then you should choose the predetermined standard system.

If you have at least some idea about which services should be available in your system and which should not, it would be best to use the compact selection. If, on the other hand, you want to assemble a completely individual system and you are acquainted with Linux software packages, you should go for the series installation or individual selection.

Determining the services by compact selection

In each of these cases there is a predetermined essential minimum basic system, which can be extended by selecting additional software packages. The minimum will normally include the X Window system as well as documentation and a development environment. You will be in need of the development environment as soon as you want to generate a kernel tailor made for your hardware.

Base system serves as a foundation

When selecting the software packages you really should choose neither the maximum system nor all available packages at once. Modern hard disks will surely provide more than enough space for a maximum system, but as a rule you should go for quality rather than quantity. The only good reason to install all available packages is to test alternatives. If you do this then you can remove the less desirable alternatives with the RPM mechanism.

It's quality not quantity that counts!

You would be better to start with installing the series and areas with which you are acquainted already or those which you know for certain that you will really use. Then you can extend your system step by step.

Extending the system step by step

This "slim" system also gives you a much better overview than the maximum system. For many packages it only makes sense to choose one from a list of similar packages (e.g. newsreader or editors).

Rapid orientation

There are several packages of the same type mainly for the purpose of being able to meet the individual demands of every single user. By proceeding step by step it will be much easier to understand when and where the packages find their place in the system.

Individual demands

POWER LINUX has comprehensive mechanisms which make it possible to determine exactly when each software package has been installed. This also makes it easier to remove existing packages from the system.

3.9.1 Compact Selection

Selection by areas of application

In comparison to the series selection, the compact selection makes it easier to decide exactly which software packages to choose. It gives you the possibility of extending the basic system with following areas:

- developer system,

- documentation,

- games and entertainment,

- text editors,

- network support,

- use as a server,

- X Window system.

Areas of application

Each area is again divided in a number of sub-areas of application, which are offered then in a second complete menu. From this menu you can make a selection that exactly meets the intended application purposes of your Linux system.

Depending on the individual selection made in the first menu, subsequent application areas will be offered. For example, for the X Window System area you can select:

- applications for X11,

- developer system for X11,

- Emacs for X11,

- extensions to X11.

You can not choose between single software packages. You can see how much space is needed for the selected modules and check how much space remains available on the target partitions. In general you should always leave some additional space ($¿$ 15 MB) as leeway.

3.9.2 The Series Selection

Subdivision in single series

If you go for the series selection, you are first presented with a selection of all available POWER LINUX series. Within each of these series you have a number of single software packages that you can choose from.

Before getting the list of the single software packages you get the opportunity to pre-select a certain proportion of these packages.

You can pre-select the necessary minimum, a recommended compilation or all the packages. After having decided on one of the pre-selection level you have the chance to choose single packages by marking them (x) with the space bar, and you can also remove this mark by pressing the space bar again.

Mark with (x)

Packages marked by a hash (#) cannot be removed, as they are vital parts for the function of your Linux system. Trying to install a system without the basic packages would like trying to drive a car without wheels.

*Vital packages are
marked by (#)*

Press the **F2** key to see a description of the currently highlighted package. Having made an individual selection, return to the main menu of the additional series by pressing **Return**.

*Comprehensive
description with F2*

When choosing the X Window system be sure to choose the appropriate X server for your graphics card. Usually it doesn't make much sense to choose several X servers. To be on the safe side the X-mono server should be installed as it can be used with almost every graphics card without problem.

*Choosing the
appropriate X
server*

Within the main menu of the series selection you can see how much hard disk space is needed for the packages already chosen, and how much space is still left on the target partitions used for the installation.

Furthermore, during the installation of the single packages you get current information on the package to be installed and on how much hard disk space is still available. This is so you are always informed about the remaining capacity of your hard disk and can orientate yourself when choosing the packages.

When you have chosen all series and packages desired and have still enough hard disk space (> 15 MB) at your disposal, then you can leave the preselection with the item "installation of the chosen software packages".

*Leave sufficient
free space*

3.9.3   Installation of the Selected Software Packages

The individual packages are now installed according to your selection. This process runs automatically if the complete POWER LINUX data are on the installation source. During this automatic installation which, on slow computers, can last up to an hour, you can allow yourself a fine cup of tea. The online help supports you with valuable tips on the topic "tea".

*Automatic
installation*

If you receive an update to LST 2.2 in the form of fix-diskettes, after the package installation has finished you have the opportunity to install these diskettes. You will be asked whether or not you want to install fix-diskettes. Go for "yes" only if you really have received such diskettes.

Fix-diskettes

Feel free to visit us at "www.lst.de" and check out if there have been updates or innovations. In this way we can provide you with the latest drivers and kernel sources.

3.10   System Configuration

Concluding configuration of the system

You have now installed all desired software packages on the hard disk. What's very important now is configuring of the system to meet your demands and the existing hardware.

In this procedure LISA modifies one system file after another is adapted. If you call up LISA later on, you can change specific system files.

The questions you are asked when adapting the system are mostly answered by themselves. If there are uncertainties you can at any time call up an additional help with **F1**.

Creation of system and index files

Having answered all questions on the configuration certain index files are installed, such as the database for the manual pages or the teTeX font table. Depending on the size of the installed system, this process can last several minutes.

3.10.1   The Network Configuration

Do completely carry out the network configuration

In case the network series has been part of your software selection, LISA will carry out a network configuration. It must be carried out completely at least once for the network features of POWER LINUX to be correctly configured.

Introduction to networking – Chap. 7

Of course you can call up the network configuration again via LISA at any time, e.g. if your system has been changed. In Chap. 7 you will find an introduction on the basics of networks which helps you to answer your questions on network configuration.

3.10.2   The Boot Configuration

In the "boot process" area of LISA you can determine the way in which your Linux system is to be started after power-on.

The Linux Loader can do more than just loading Linux

As you already know, an operating system must be loaded into the main memory before it can be started. The reason for the name LILO ("LInux LOader") is that it is responsible for loading a Linux kernel into the main memory. Although it isn't obvious from the name LILO can also load and start other operating systems, such as DOS.

The LILO boot menu can give you a selection of several operating systems and, in the case of Linux, also makes it possible to pass additional boot parameters to the Linux kernel.

Choice in the LILO boot menu

At this point the various possibilities that the menu of the POWER LINUX boot manager offers can be explained in concrete terms. Every operating system known to LISA gets a boot label by which it can be refered to in the boot manager. So at boot time, when the boot manager runs, you need only state the name of the operating system you want loaded into main memory.

The four different possibilities of using LILO are offered in the "boot process..." area by LISA. They are shown in the following table:

Different boot variants

	1	2	3	4
kernel	diskette	diskette	hard disk	hard disk
LILO	–	diskette	diskette	hard disk

Possibilities 1 to 4 are explained below. You can see in the table where the respective kernel or LILO is located.

Option 1: Linux Kernel on a Diskette

When choosing this option the Linux kernel is installed directly on the diskette by the **dd** command. As no LILO is installed, there is no boot menu and no possibility of transfering parameters to the kernel when booting with this diskette.

Only the Linux kernel on the diskette

Option 2: Boot Diskette with LILO

On the whole, this method provides the most secure solution. Both LILO and the kernel image are copied onto the diskette. Although the boot process needs more time than it would if the kernel image was on the hard disk, you avoid the risk of not finding the kernel image when, for example the partitioning of the hard disk has been changed.

Linux kernel and LILO on the diskette

Option 3: LILO on a Diskette

If LILO cannot or should not be installed on the hard disk this possibility is a good alternative. In this case LILO is installed on a diskette, the kernel image, though, remains on the hard disk.

Only LILO on the diskette

With this method the boot process hardly needs more time than the booting from the hard disk, because only the first sector from the diskette must be read in. This contains LILO with all necessary information on where the bootable Linux kernel or alternative operating systems are to be found on the hard disk.

Almost as quick as from the hard disk

Option 4: LILO on a hard disk

This is the most elegant and also the quickest way of booting. LILO and the kernel image are located on the hard disk. This alternative is safest when LILO is installed on the first hard disk on a primary partition. It is simplest to install LILO in the boot sector of the partition on which your Linux root file system is located. Don't try installing LILO into a DOS or OS/2 primary partition.

Linux kernel and LILO on the hard disk

- Installing LILO in the root partition

Booting directly from a primary partition of the first hard disk

When your Linux root partition is located on the first hard disk of your computer, this partition is proposed automatically. If your Linux partition isn't located on the first hard disk, you can in fact install LILO in the boot sector of your root partition, but not use it for booting directly. LILO always has to be installed on a primary partition of the first hard disk if you want to boot directly with it.

Booting via a second LILO boot manager

Nevertheless, you can help yourself with a small trick to make Linux boot directly from the hard disk. To achieve this, you install another LILO boot manager on a primary partition of the first hard disk. From there you can start the LILO boot loader of your Linux root partition on another hard disk.

There are two methods of installing LILO on the first hard disk, whilst the root partition is located on the second hard disk:

- Install LILO on a primary partition of the first hard disk

LILO in its own mini-partition

We cannot decide which partition to use for you. Perhaps you still have enough still space to do something similar to what OS/2 does with its OS/2 Boot Manager, namely to create a small Linux partition on the first hard disk, which only serves the purpose of holding LILO.

We can also recommend the possibility of using another Linux partition, which doesn't contain a root file system, for LILO (e.g. the partition, which you mount at **/archiv** in the file system).

Under no circumstances should you choose a swap partition for LILO

But under no circumstances should you install LILO on a swap partition or on the boot partition of another operating system: LILO would be completely overwritten when the swap partition is actived or LILO itself would overwrite the boot information of the foreign operating system.

No matter which partition you specify for the LILO installation, LILO will use the boot sector of this partition for itself and thus overwrite it.

- Install LILO in the MBR of the first hard disk

If no existing partition of the first hard disk can be used for the installation of LILO, the last resort is to install LILO in the Master Boot Record (MBR) of the first hard disk.

Use the MBR cautiously!

We do not recommend this and warn you against choosing this option! You should consider very carefully if you really want to overwrite the master boot record, as it can contain the partition table, perhaps a list of defective sectors, and further important data on the hard disk, like for example the translation of physical to logical heads, tracks, and cylinders.

The MBR contains important information about the hard disk

By installing LILO on the MBR you run the risk of possibly loosing the access to your hard disk forever.

Please note that there is a difference between the boot sector of a partition and the master boot record of a hard disk. The boot sector of a "foreign" partition can, under certain circumstances, be overwritten and used for LILO, without coming to any permanent harm, as it usually is located at the beginning of a partition and is separated from the respective file system.

Difference between the boot sector and the MBR

In comparison the MBR is responsible for the complete hard disk and therefore would be better not overwritten by LILO. In principle, though, it is possible to install LILO on the MBR without causing any harm.

3.10.3 Marking a Partition as "active"

After having decided on a partition where LILO will be installed, you must make sure that this partition is marked as "active".

If you decide to use a logical partition within the extended partition, i.e. a partition with a number over 5, for LILO and the root partition, then there must be an active boot manager already on one of the primary partitions. This is comparable to the situation with two hard disks described above.

Logical partition

This boot manager can of course be a further LILO or an existing OS/2 Boot Manager, to which you just have to introduce the Linux root partition in order to be able to boot Linux.

Using the OS/2 Boot Manager

Activating with fdisk

You can use **fdisk** to find out whether or not the partition intended for the location LILO is marked as active. In **fdisk** you can toggle a partition between being active or inactive with the **a** command.

Normally LISA will activate the right partitions, but ask before actaully doing it for confirmation.

If you carefully followed the instructions up to now, you should be able to start Linux directly from LILO the next time you boot.

Checking the boot configuration by restarting the system

Now you have completed the configuration of the system. You can either start to work with your new system or reboot first to make sure that the new boot configuration of the hard disk really works. If you want more information on rebooting, turn to the next chapter, which begins with exactly this topic.

Chapter 4

The Linux System in Operation

Practical interaction with your new Linux system starts at the end of installation. However, at some stage you will also want to quit from your Linux system and switch off your computer. What is the best way to exit the system?

To start the story from the end...

We have already stressed more than once that it is not a good idea to simply switch off the computer. For this reason we begin this chapter about interaction with Linux at the end, that is, either the reboot or shutdown of the system.

4.1 Shutting Down the Linux System Correctly

Linux uses the block buffer cache very intensively while transfering data between various devices. Should data be read from, say, the hard disk, then the kernel checks whether the data sought is already in the block buffer cache. If this is the case then the data do not have to be fetched from the hard disk and are therefore available much faster.

Block buffer cache

This principle is also used in the opposite direction. Should data be written to the hard disk, then they first transfer to the block buffer cache. From there the data are first written to the hard disk when the next hard disk access activity offers itself. If the data is changed again before it has been written to the hard disk, then the data in the block buffer cache is changed, hence saving hard disk access.

Hard disk access only as required

Normally, data which from the point of view of the user should have already been written to the hard disk, is temporarily stored in the block buffer cache to enhance performance.

Switch the computer off while it is in this state and the data will be lost. In the worst case the filesystem itself is brought into an inconsistant state and yet further data is lost or destroyed.

Danger of data loss

sync synchronises
the hard disk with
the memory

The **sync** command can be used manually at any time to ensure that the data currently in the buffer are immediately transfered to the hard disk. The system automatically runs this command every 30 seconds.

If a situation in which the system refuses to react to all input does arise, then wait these 30 seconds before you press the reset button.[1]

There are essentially three methods available to cleanly and completely finish the session with your Linux system:

- **reboot** shuts down the computer and starts it afresh,

- **shutdown** shuts down the computer and halts it, after which you can switch off the computer,

- **CTRL-ALT-DEL** (the infamous three finger salute) runs the **reboot** command, even when you are not logged in at the time.

Reboot restarts
the system

When you enter **reboot** all running processes are sent a signal telling them to abandon their work. Subsequently the processes which continue running receive a **kill** signal which terminates them forcibly. The system then executes a cold start and once again you should find yourself presented with the LILO boot menu.

shutdown brings
the system to a halt

The **shutdown** command is the one used to bring the system to a complete halt. As this method is intended for environments where there are multiple users working with the system the default action is to send all users a message warning of the impending shutdown and to delay the actual shutdown 5 minutes. This gives the users the opportunity to end their work and log out.

On the other hand if you are working alone on your computer then append the options **-h now** to **shutdown** in order to stop the system immediately.

System halted

The procedure is exactly the same as with **reboot**, with the exception that your computer does not restart, but rather stops in a stable condition. You recognise this by the message **system halted**. Now you may switch off your computer without worries.

4.2   Starting the System in Emergencies

Now that you know how to safely shutdown your Linux system we will also give you a little advice as to how to resume your work just as reliably.

---

[1] While this never actually happens with a correctly configured system, during the configuration of a new X server the graphics card may hang and although the system lives on, the screen and keboard are blocked. When you can't login from outside via a network connection, then the only remaining option is the reset button.

If you should get into a situation in which you can't boot from the hard disk and you don't have a specially made Linux boot diskette at hand, then the POWER LINUX installation diskette can be used as an emergency boot diskette for an existing Linux system.

The first aid kit for booting

By booting with the installation diskette you can gain access to your Linux system installed on the hard disk in order to repair it after a crash or power failure, for example.

To use this recovery technique, enter **boot** at the installation dis-kette's boot prompt instead of entering **install** or simply pressing **RETURN**.

LILO boot label "boot"

A further boot parameter **root=/dev/...** must be appended to specify the Linux root partition. Also, the parameter **ro** informs the filesystem check program that the root partition must at first be mounted in read only mode. An example would be:

ro parameter

```
boot ro root=/dev/hda6
```

If you forget the **ro** parameter you will see a few warnings from the filesystem check program as the check should actually be used on a root partition mounted for reading and writing.

4.3 Logging In and Out

A significant feature of Linux is its ability to manage multiple users using the system simultaneously. In order to distinguish these individ-ual users from each other, every user registers with the system at the beginning of his or her working session.

Multiple users

4.3.1 The `login:` Prompt

If your first contact with Unix is the Linux system before you, then you are justified in asking what purpose this **login:** prompt serves.

Login, passwort and what next?

As you previously read, Linux is not only a multitasking operating system (i.e multiple programs can run largely independently of each other), but also a multiuser operating system. This means that Linux brings with it all those prerequisites which allow numerous users to work simultaneously, but nevertheless independently.

Multi-user system

You may now exclaim that the multiuser capabilities of your com-puter are severely limited due to the fact that has only one monitor and one keyboard attached. This is of course true in most cases, but it doesn't have to remain so. Above all else Linux shines in network operation.

Remote logins

Multiple terminals

Sequential usage

*No access to other
users' files*

*A home for
every user*

*The home
directory*

Connect your computer with a network card and cables to other computers and **remote** users working on the other computers will be able to log in to your computer.

The connection of additional terminals to your computer via its serial interfaces is equally conceivable. From these terminals other users can log into your system whenever it is running. This type of connection can also be achieved through a modem.

A home computer will rarely have simultaneous users, but it is conceivable that it will be used by a number of people at various times during the week. Consider that a family member or friend may want to work with Linux on your computer while you are out for the evening.

For all these situations the same problem exists. As soon as more than one person works on a single computer there is the danger that one user could access, perhaps alter or even delete files belonging to the other users.

A multiuser operating system has a solution for precisely this problem: every user of the system works independently of others in their own private area of the filesystem. Within their private area each user can determine for themselves which data they permit other users to access and the level of access permitted. This ensures that each user has their own private sphere.

The private area for each user is his or her home directory, also called "home" for short. When the user logs in, his home directory is automatically made the current working directory. The home directory is usually located under **home** as shown in Fig. 4.1.

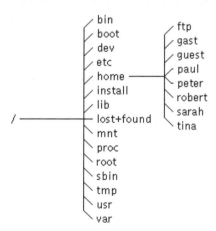

Fig. 4.1: The location of the home directory in the filesystem.

In his home directory the user has permission to create files or modify files. Usually he also has permission to read files in most parts of the system, but for reasons of security cannot alter these parts.

Write permission in
the home directory

4.3.2 The Superuser

Permission to alter the system setup is reserved for a special user of the system: the system administrator, also known as the superuser or **root** for short. **root** is the name the superuser uses to log into the system.

The system
administrator - root

The superuser is responsible for ensuring that the system runs problem free at all times. She installs and tests new software for the users and takes care of providing the users with the storage space that they require.

System
management

At this point you will be probably asking: great, so where do I find my personal superuser? It will probably already have dawned on you that the superuser was not supplied in the box with the CD-ROM as part of the standard package. You have to take over this roll yourself; you are responsible for ensuring that your system works. This is really not as bad as it sounds. After all don't you want to learn something about Linux and to gain experience using it?

So that the transition into the life of a system administrator isn't too tough, we have provided you with a friendly assistant to help in your work as system administrator. Ready at your right hand is: LISA.

LISA can relieve you of many of the details of system administration when you wish. Naturally you are free to do all that is necessary by hand, but this means one must become confident in all aspects of basic system administration, i.e. one must learn much more. This can be seen as an advantage.

LISA takes care
of the details

You have already had your first experience with LISA during installation. Be honest, would you have really enjoyed doing the installation by hand? So you see, a good adiministration tool has its advantages.

In order to be able to undertake absolutely any alteration to the system, the system administrator **root** has unlimited access to the whole system. The other side of this coin is that with the unlimited permission to alter anything and everything mistakes made by the superuser can cause serious damage to the system.

Unlimited access
to the system

For this reason you should only undertake system administration tasks as **root** when really necessary. Always take your first steps with Linux as a normal user. As a normal user you cannot cause too much havoc. This brings us to the first task for LISA: you need to create a new user.

Only use the power
of the superuser
login when
necessary

First you must inform the system that the superuser wants to get into action. As you already know the system indicates that it is ready to let users work by displaying the **login:** prompt.

Bash

When you want to work as superuser then login as user **root**. After logging in you see the prompt of the Bash (Bourne Again SHell). Bash is the standard shell for Linux and is in principle a very comprehensive command line interpreter. It executes all the valid commands that you enter.

If you don't know any Unix commands at all, then please get your hands on an introductory Unix book and become familiar with the basic concepts and commands.

lisa

For the task at hand it suffices to know that LISA is run with the command **lisa**. Once LISA is running, move into the area "System Administration..." and from there into the menu "User Administration...". In Fig. 4.2 you see LISA's User Administration window.

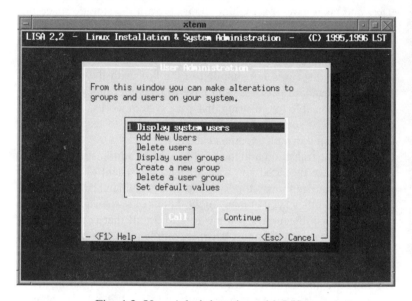

Fig. 4.2: User Administration with LISA.

*Creating a
new user*

Select the item "Create new user..." and enter the data for the new user. Along with details about the user LISA also wants a password for them.

4.3.3   The Password

*The password –
the security ID
of each user*

But why does every user need to have a password? Actually it is only needed for security and to ensure that the user is who they say they are. What prevents one user from pretending to be another at login, prying about in that users' private directories or creating havoc? It is the password that prevents this sort of undesirable behaviour.

The password is the key to user authentication for Unix. The password is therefore very important. It should not be written down where it may be discovered and it should also be very difficult to guess or crack.

While thinking up a password it is worthwhile bearing in mind that upper and lowercase letters are distinguished and that the use of digits and special characters greatly enhances the your password's resistance to password cracking programs.

Best of all think out an acronym for a password. At first glance the password **OfAaAf1!** would be extremely difficult to guess or to crack. Nonetheless you will be able to easily remember this password as long as you remember the line "One for all and all for one!". Well, it's easy for you and all the others who read this book - so don't use this password.

The significance of the password depends largely on how your system is used. You could deduce from our cautious attitude that we find ourselves working within large networks in which password security is of the utmost importance.

When you are definitely the only user of your system (perhaps because the rest of the family or your collegues haven't acquired a taste for Linux) and nobody is likely to want to snoop in your files, then you can forget about the password.

As soon as more than one person works with the computer, or the computer is connected to the Internet or another network from time to time (e.g. through a modem) you should really ensure that all users have a secure password. Above all, **root** should have a good password.

If an outsider manages to gain entry into your system, they have the opportunity to cause damage in a wide variety of ways. This can begin with discovering the passwords of other users and end with your whole hard disk being freshly formatted.

But let's return to our original task - creating a new user on the system. If in the long run many people will be using the system you should consider assigning the usernames according to some scheme. This can simply be the first or last names of the user and could also be combined with a project or department name. So that uniqueness is also maintained with surnames like "Smith" the surame can be combined with the first names.

The user "Gerald Smith" could be assigned the username **gdsmith** (the first and last letters of the first name plus the last name). Alternatively he could have **gm** (his initials) when your system only has a few users.

Always use lower case letters for usernames. A username may not contain special characters and must begin with a letter.

Naturally every new system user requires his or her own password. After you have thought of a suitably difficult password, such as

"Mouse", "Linux" or "Sabina" this is now entered in LISA. It is left as an exercise for the user to dream up their own tricky password. After you have responded to LISA's remaining questions about the user, you can exit from LISA.

Test the new login

Switch to another virtual console (with **ALT-F2** for example) and enter the username of the new user at the login prompt. You will then be prompted for the user's password which you have remembered, hopefully.

If the username you entered does not exist or the password you gave is wrong then the login prompt will appear again. In this case the system denied you access. Try again.

4.4   The First Steps

The command prompt

Once you have given the username and password correctly, the shell command prompt appears as did it after logging as root. You may notice that the shell command prompt is no longer the **#** as it was for the system administrator, but rather a $. For example, for Sarah working on the system "excite" as the user "sarah":

```
sarah@excite:~$
```

A **#** indicates that you are logged in as the system administrator and reminds you that you should be appropriately cautious as you work, because as **root** there are no limits as to what you can do to the system.

pwd - print working directory

After logging in as a normal user you find that the current working directory is your home directory. You can always display your current working directory with the command **pwd** (print working directory).

```
sarah@excite:~$ pwd
/home/sarah
sarah@excite:~$
```

The **who** command instructs your computer to list all the users who are currently logged in.

```
sarah@excite:~$ who
root        tty1       Jul 30 10:57
sarah       tty2       Jul 30 15:04
sarah@excite:~$
```

Tell me who I am

In our case the **root** and the new username you created should be listed. With the commands **id** (identity), **whoami** (who am I), and **tty** you orient yourself with respect to who you originally logged in as and which console you are currently working on.

```
sarah@excite:~$ id
uid=1234(sarah) gid=100(users) groups=100(users)
sarah@excite:~$ whoami
sarah
sarah@excite:~$
```

What you can't see from the output of the **whoami** command is, that Sarah first logged in as **root** then later switched to "sarah" with the command **su sarah**. The superuser can take on the identity of any user with the **su** command. A normal user can also do this, but then requires the associated password.[2]

To find out what the users are currently up to in the system enter the command **w** (what) or **ps -aux** (process status with all users and other information).

What's happening at the moment?

```
sarah@excite:~$ w
 3:19pm up 4:23, 7 users, load average: 0.00, 0.01, 0.03
  User    tty     login@  idle   JCPU   PCPU   what
  root    tty1    10:57am  1                    -
  sarah   tty2    3:04pm   9                    -
sarah@excite:~$
```

The commands **ls** (list) and **dir** display the contents of the working directory, and with the command **cd Directory-Name** you can change your working directory to the one specified.

Directory list

```
sarah@excite:~$ ls
Mail     archiv  doc      source  text    work
sarah@excite:~$
```

Many users ask why **ls** doesn't produce color coded output by default after installation. There is a good reason. In order to assign the appropriate color the type of each file must be determined, but unlike under DOS, the type cannot just simply be assumed from the filename extention. File typing under Unix involves looking into each file to see what it contains i.e. a considerable amount of work. Particularly when you are using an NFS filesystem, the extra load this places on the system is too great to make it part of a sensible default setup.

Color coded directory lists

Nevertheless, the simplest way of getting a color coded directory list is to append the **-o** option to **ls** or to define an alias for **ls**. Aliases will be covered a little later.

Note that X11's standard **xterm** doesn't support colors. The extended **ansi_xterm** does support colors and is used for example when LISA is run in X11.

xterm
ansi_xterm

---

[2] The **su -** command i.e. **su** followed by a minus sign has the same effect as a login with the exception that one was already logged in.

Attention! /
instead of \

Changing the
working directory

Before we move on to changing the working directory, please note that Unix pathnames are joined with the slash / and not with the backslash \ as under DOS.[3]

To change the working directory to the highest level of the directory tree enter the command **cd /** and then from there become acquainted with the directory **/usr/doc**. Most of your Linux system documentation is located in **/usr/doc**. E.g.:

```
root@excite:~# cd /usr/doc
root@excite:/usr/doc# ls LDP
igs-2.2.2  khg-0.6   lpg-0.4   nag-1.0   sag-0.3   ug-0.4
root@excite:/usr/doc#
```

Check file type

The most interesting documents to be found there are the Linux HOWTOs and FAQs. These are also viewable from LISA's help system.

Before you try viewing a file it is a good idea to check out what type of file it is with the command **file Filename** to be sure that it is what you expect.

```
root@excite:/usr/doc/FAQ# file linux-faq.ascii
linux-faq.ascii: English text
root@excite:/usr/doc/FAQ#
```

The wildcard
symbol *

To check on all the files in a directory in one hit, then instead of given a particular filename use the * wildcard symbol. The shell automatically expands the * to all filenames in the current directory, with the result that the **file** command is run with all the filenames in the directory one after the other.

```
root@excite:/usr/doc/FAQ# file *
LILO-FAQ.gz:         gzip compressed data
NFS-FAQ.gz:          gzip compressed data
Wine.FAQ.gz:         gzip compressed data
ext2fs-FAQ.gz:       gzip compressed data
linux-faq.ascii:     English text
linux-faq.ascii.gz:  gzip compressed data
linux-faq.ps.gz:     gzip compressed data
root@excite:/usr/doc/FAQ#
```

---

[3] Even Microsoft would have liked to use the / as the path separator if it had not already been prematurely reserved for the command option prefix. After it was recognised that a single directory is in fact somewhat limiting, the structured directory was also introduced to DOS. By that time only the similar \ remained as a suitable choice.

To display the content of a file you can use the **cat** command. **cat** gives the content out all at once, which for some purposes is useful, but not if you want to read long files as you only see their tail ends.

The command **less** is a cure for this problem. **less** allows you to view the text file page for page. **more** is more or less the same as **less**, except that **more** ends itself automatically when it reaches the end of a file. Both commands allow you to page forward with **f** or the spacebar and back again with **b**. The **/** command allows you to search for a particular pattern. The quit command is **q**.

Paging through text files with less

Files that have been compressed to save space can be recognized by their **.gz** ending. To view these files use the **zcat** command instead of **cat**. The command line **zcat Filename | less** first unpacks the file (**zcat**) then pushes the data through a pipe (**|**) on to the **less** command. The pipe creates a connection between two commands.

Compressed files

The same result is achieved by simply using the **zless** command and saves you typing the **|**.

zless

4.4.1 Quick Help

A Unix or Linux system may have hundreds of commands and the commands may have numerous options. If you are not sure how a command can be used or you want to see all of a commands option then use the command **man Command_Name** to display the Manual Page for the command.

Manual Pages

You should make youself very familar with the **man** command as there are comprehensive man pages for almost all commands and system files.

man

You don't know the exact name of the command you need? The **apropos Name** command will list all the commands known to man which contain the pattern "Name" and those whose short description contains "Name". If on the other hand you know the command, but can't remember what it does then the command **whatis Command_Name** is the one you need.

Apropos

4.4.2 Path Problems

Many users become confused in the situation where they want to run a program which is in the working directory,

```
roger@lisa:/usr/lib/apsfilter-4.9$ ls
SETUP  bin    doc    filter  global  setup  template
roger@lisa:/usr/lib/apsfilter-4.9$ SETUP
```

but instead of running the program the shell only reports

```
bash: SETUP: command not found
roger@lisa:/usr/lib/apsfilter-4.9$ SETUP
```

The PATH variable

The problem lies in the fact that although the program **SETUP** is in the working directory, the working directory is not in your path list. When you want to run a command the shell searches for this command in all the directories whose paths are listed your by **$PATH** variable.

Current directory is not in the path variable

The current directory is traditionally not listed in the path variable for system security reasons. Hence in the example above the shell cannot find the program **SETUP** so it gives out an error message. The value of the path variable can be displayed to see which directories are searched for commands:

```
roger@lisa:/usr/lib/apsfilter-4.9$ echo $PATH
/sbin:/usr/sbin:/usr/bin:/bin:/usr/X11R6/bin:/usr/TeX/bin:
                /usr/openwin/bin:~/bin
```

As you can see the current working directory**/usr/lib/aps-filter-4.9** is not in your path variable.

Caution – Impostor danger!

A worse problem can occur when a completely different program is run in place of the one you intended. This program has the same name as the one you wanted to run, but may produce a completely different result. This situation can also occur when a identically named command exists on a path in the path variable before the path to the command you actually want. The shell searchs the value of path variable from left to right.

Positioning within the path variable value is not the only cause of such misunderstandings:

Alias

- An alias. Aliases define substitute names for commands to save typing. They are usually defined so they have the same name as the original command, plus some options. The **rm** (remove file) command is a good example to bring to your attention.

  The command sequence **rm -i** is often given the alias **rm** for use by system administrator or normal users. The option **i** instructs the **rm** command to prompt the user for comfirmatiom before erasing files. Whenever the **rm Filename** command is used while this alias is set, the shell first replaces the **rm** with **rm -i**.[4]

---

[4] Don't make assumptions about the aliasing of **rm** on a new system, especially if you are the working as the superuser, as there are differing opinions about its default setting.

- Hashing. The shell has a mechanism which keeps a log of where a command was last found. The intention of this mechanism is to reduce the time taken to find and start running a command. This mechanism is named "hashing" after the technique used to maintain the log table.

  Hashing

  An example: the first time you run the command **list** after you log in, the shell finds this command in the directory **/usr/local/bin** and logs this fact. The next time you run **list** the shell finds the **/usr/local/bin/list** in its hash table before it starts searching through the contents of path variables again.

  An internal shortcut

  You get a error message when, in the meantime, you have re-named, moved or erased the command even though the command may still exist in one of the directories in the path variable. This happens because the shell attempts to run the now invalid hash table entry. The problem is cured by running **hash -r** to rebuild the hash table.

  hash -r

The **which** command is helpful in these cases. It returns the absolute path to the command that the shell would attempt to use if you entered the command without any path.

which

```
roger@lisa:~$ which rm
/bin/rm
```

It is easiest to avoid such path related problems by always using the absolute or full pathname for commands outside the working directory and by typing **./** before the program name for programs in the working directory.

```
roger@lisa:~$ /usr/lib/apsfilter-4.9/SETUP
```

or

```
roger@lisa:/usr/lib/apsfilter-4.9$ ./SETUP
```

The question is whether or not one will remember this tip at the critical time.

Although there is definitely enough scope for many more pages on these themes we will move on to a new topic at this point. We recommend instead that you obtain one of the innumerable introductory Unix books which thoroughly explain Unix with the help of many examples.

4.5 The X Window System

Graphical interface

The X Window System graphical user interface, also refered to as X11 or X, from the Massachusetts Institute of Technology (MIT) is widely used in the Unix world (Fig. 4.3). The strength of the X Window System lies in its complete network support. Graphical applications can be run transparently across the network.

X11 server

The only prerequisite is that an X server has to run on each computer on which X11 services should be available. The X server is a program which provides the X11 functionality and controls the graphics card.

Programs which are installed on another computer and which are not available on your Linux computer, either because they don't run directly under Linux or you simply have not installed them, can be used on your Linux computer. These must either be terminal based programs which will run in an Xterm, or X Window programs.

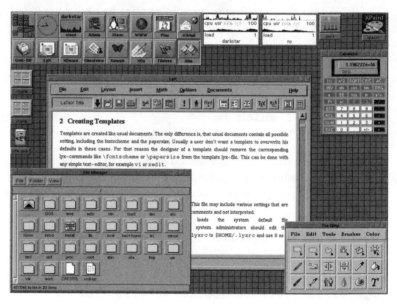

Fig. 4.3: The X Window System with the FVWM window manager.

Using programs over the network

For example, assume that there is a Sun workstation in your network and Adobe Photoshop is installed on it. This program is not directly available for Linux, but you can redirect its output windows onto your Linux computer.

Output windows are drawn locally

These output windows are constructed according to the characteristics and color depth defined by the settings of your Linux X server. You can use the program just as if it were running directly on your Linux computer. Depending on the type of network in use, the display performance will be subject to imperceptible delays or noticeable lags as the X server and the X client, i.e. the application program, need to continually exchange data.

Additionaly, a network wide access control can permit or refuse a program the right to display output on the X servers display on a per user or per host computer basis. This access control can also be on an all or none basis.

Network wide access control

The X Window System represents a logical extension of the Unix concept into the graphical user interface. The look and feel of the graphics interface is not determined by X11, but rather by the Window manager chosen. Most Linux distributions use a common Window manager: FVWM, which we will discuss in more detail later.

Still no uniform operation

XFree86™ is a freely available version of the X Window system and therefore it is uniformly used in most Linux distributions. Aside from the Linux PC platform it is also available for a number of other operating systems, such as NetBSD, FreeBSD, Mach, Amoeba and SVR4.

XFree86

XFree86 is available in the versions 2 and 3, where version 2.1.1 is based on X11R5 and version 3.2.x is based on the newer X11R6(.1). X11R5 is essentially no longer used for Linux. The version you need to use depends mostly on whether or not you have special software which only runs under either X11R5 or X11R6.

X11R6

If you use a newer graphics card you must use XFree86 3.2.x, as only this version is able to support the modern cards.

Unfortunately, there are still a number of graphics cards which are not supported sufficiently by XFree86, or which cause some problems in the interaction with XFree86. This is very often the case with leading edge graphics cards.

Not all graphics cards are supported

If you definitely have problems with XFree86, the only alternative is to buy one of the commercial X servers for Linux. On the POWER LINUX CD-ROM we included a demo version of Accelerated X. It is limited to ten minutes running time, just enough time to find out whether it supports the graphics card at all.

Commercial X Server

Besides a broader range of support for new graphics cards, the commercial X servers mostly offer much better performance, as compensation for the relatively high price. The two best known products are Metro X from Metro Link and Accelerated X from X Inside. As a hint we recommend Caldera Network Desktop or Caldera Open Linux, which includes either Accelerated X or Metro X as a standard component, but costs barely more than a commercial X server alone.

High performance and high prices
Metro X

Accelerated X

Before explaining more precisely how to operate the X Window systems, we will first give you some help configuring XFree86 and using it efficiently.

4.6   Configuration of XFree86

*Direct hardware
access*

The configuration of XFree86 isn't that simple because the X server directly programmes the existing hardware in order to be able to use it as efficiently as possible. Since there is great variation in the required settings we cannot supply you with a preconfigured X11 system that operates correctly and efficiently with each and every hardware configuration.

*Minimal
configuration file*

We follow instead the advice of "The XFree86 Project, Inc" and just provide you with an example configuration file. This serves as a starting point for your own individual configuration. You will notice that

*Individual
configuration*

the individual configuration is worthwhile. The performance reached by XFree86 with a simple ET4000 graphics card is really quite astonishing.

*Documentation
for XFree86*

First of all you should cast a glance at the documentation for XFree86. All directories and files relevant to X11R6, are in the directory **/usr/X11R6**. The documentation for X11 is to be found under **/usr/X11R6/lib/X11/doc**.

Some READMEs about the particulars of certain graphics cards are also located there. There is also a HOWTO for XFree86 to be found under **/usr/doc/HOWTO/XFree86-HOWTO**.

*Manual pages
for XFree86*

You should also glance at the manual pages for **X** (the X11 server), **XFree86** (general information on XFree86), **xf86config** (the configuration program for XFree86), **reconfig** (the program for converting existing **XConfig** files) and **XF86Config** (the XFree86 configuration file).

VideoModes.doc

You should in any case read the file **VideoModes.doc**, which explains the basics of video timings and the setting of your graphics card to the monitor. It also explains how to proceed in order to attain the best performance from your graphics card and monitor. But do proceed with the utmost care; a bad setting can cause harm to your graphics card or monitor.

*Arbitrary choice
of grahics chips*

Unfortunately the situation is not made easier by the fact that graphics card producers sometimes populate what appear to be virtually identical cards with completely different components. So don't blame XFree86; it is excellently programmed and tries to achieve the best with your hardware.

*Technical data of
your hardware*

To be able to configure XFree86 you need the technical data about your monitor, as well as documents on your graphics card with information about the chipset, the clockchip, and the amount of video memory on the card. It is also very useful to know the video modes for your monitor. They can often be found in the file **modeDB.txt**.

XF86Config

Every XFree86 server gets its configuration from the central file **/usr/X11R6/lib/X11/XF86Config** or **/etc/X11R6/ XF86Config**, depending on the installation. It is important to set this configuration file properly. After installation, there will only be the file **XF86Config.eg**, which contains an example **XF86Config** file.

The file **XF86Config** consists of several "sections" to be filled with information on your hardware.

Sections

The sections are:

- files section; the paths to the most important system files are stated here, such as the X11 font sets and color definitions;

- server flags section, where you can enter special options (flags) for the respective X server;

- keyboard section, where the keyboard setting is determined;

- pointer section, where the mouse type and the mouse protocol are entered;

- monitor section; which contains technical information on the monitor. If several monitors are used this section can also be entered several times;

- graphics device section, where the data for the graphics card are entered. If there are several graphics cards each one gets its own section;

- screen sections; a complete configuration of X11 is set there by combining references to the sections above.

By administrating the hardware data precisely, XFree86 can provide a basic protection function. If a maximum line scanning frequency of, say, 64 KHz is set, the X server won't permit a graphics resolution which results in a line scanning frequency higher than 64 KHz. This hardware protection is only given when the file **XF86Config** is used properly.

Protection function

Maximum scanning line frequency

The following items are important key data for the configuration of XFree86:

- type, manufacturer, chipset, clockchip and video memory of the graphics card;

- the usage of a suitable X server for the graphics card;

- the maximum line and screen refresh frequency, as well as the bandwidth of the monitor;

- the various clock values of the graphics card;

- a number of possible video resolutions;

- the type of mouse used and its connection.

SuperProbe

But before you can determine the proper entries for your computer's **XF86Config** file, you first need some information. It is most important to know how your graphics card behaves. The **SuperProbe** program found under **/usr/X11R6/bin** can be used to determine this. Please read the **SuperProbe** manual page before starting it, as it may lockup your computer's hardware.

*Detailed
information on the
graphics card*

Call up **SuperProbe -info**, to see which graphics cards can be recognized by **SuperProbe**. Usually **SuperProbe** will then provide you with detailed information on your graphics card. We will give you the following example for a Tseng ET4000/W32 card:

```
First video:    Super-VGA
Chipset:        Tseng ET4000/W32i Rev B
Memory:         1024 Kbytes
RAMDAC:         AT&T 20C490 15/16/24-bit DAC
```

xf86config

Write down the data provided by **SuperProbe** about your graphics card. You will need this data later. The next step is to start one of the two XFree86 configuration programs **xf86config** and **XF86Setup**, which will create the **XF86Config** file for your system. Both programs are located in the directory **/usr/X11R6/bin**.

Fig. 4.4 shows the initial screen of XF86Setup.

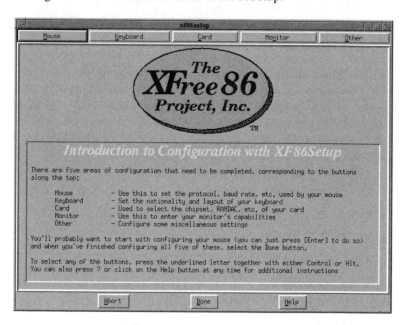

Fig. 4.4: The X Window System Setup Tool **XF86Setup**.

Since **XF86Setup** is a very convenient, self explaining tool and in principle just a graphical frontend to **xf86config**, we prefer to explain the use of the latter, as it is text based.

xf86config first checks if your path variable has been set correctly for XFree86 3.2.x, which should be the case after a new installation of POWER LINUX .

A number of settings relating to the mouse are then made. These settings are the mouse type, the emulation of a third mouse button if you have a two button mouse, the serial port, to which the mouse is connected, and the specification of the **Meta** key under X11.

Information about the mouse

Technical data on the monitor and the graphics card are requested next. Now you need information on the bandwidth and maximum line scanning frequency of the monitor, and on the chipset, the clockchip and on the amount of video RAM on the graphics card. In case your monitor handbook doesn't contain sufficient information, you may find the data sought in the monitor database **lib/X11/doc/Monitors** of XFree86.

Information on the monitor

After you have supplied the technical information on the monitor, the name, type, and the producer of the monitor are requested. The monitor is then entered under these labels within the monitor sections of **XF86Config**.

Monitor section

Before giving the technical details on your graphics card, you have the opportunity to search for your card in the graphics card database. If you find your card in the list then select it and you will be offered the chipset and the X server appropriate for this card. You should note these details, then you have to decide which X server you actually want to use. If you have found your graphics card in the database, you are offered the appropriate X server for your card.

Graphics card database

Determining the X Server

The best performance can be attained by choosing an accelerated X Server, provided that there is one for your graphics card. Note also that in order to be able to use an X server, you must have already installed it. If you haven't done this already, you can do so at any time later with the help of LISA.

Accelerated and non-accelerated X servers

The XFree86 servers are to be found in the series **xbasis**. Currently there are the following servers:

- non accelerated servers:

    XF86_Mono

    XF86_VGA16

    XF86_SVGA

- accelerated servers:

    XF86_S3

    XF86_S3V

XF86_W32

XF86_Mach8

XF86_Mach32

XF86_Mach64

XF86_P9000

XF86_AGX

XF86_8514

Technical
details on your
graphics card

For the next step you will need the details of your graphics card, which are entered then within the device section of **XF86Config**. The amount of video memory on the card, the exact label for the card, the producer of the card, the model, the RAMDAC chip and the clockchip are all called for. If possible, enter the values which are listed for your card in the graphics card database.

Clocks line

Having determined the monitor and the graphics card it is recommended that you determine a **clocks** line, in which the various clock values of your graphics card are listed. This **clocks** line isn't absolutely necessary but avoids problems when starting X11 on a loaded system and risking disruption of the X11 timing behaviour. If this prob-

System load
influences the
determination of
the clock values

lem occurs once it can occur several times until the X server is successfully started. The X server doesn't have to dynamically find out the appropriate clock timing for itself each time it starts if there is already a **clocks** line to give it the information about the graphics card's clock speeds that it requires.

Several
resolutions
possible

The graphics card can be operated at a number of different resolutions. X11 allows any resolution to be specified so long as it remains within the range defined by the hardware specifications. You can define a number of resolutions and switch between them at any time with the **ctrl-alt** and **+** or **–** keys.

Optimum display

Thanks to this freedom you can set graphic modes which achieve a maximum resolution with an optimum screen refresh rate. It is not uncommon with XFree86 to set such non-standard video resolutions as for example 760 **x** 560 pixels with an 82 Hz screen refresh rate. You can also make optimum use of 1 MB video memory with the resolution 1152 **x** 870.[5]

Limits are only set
by the hardware

As long as the monitor can cope with the resulting line frequency and the graphics card can supply accordingly high clock values, a screen refresh rate of more than 80 Hz is possible even with a 1152 x 870 resolution. The limits are determined only by the hardware, i.e. the monitor or the graphics card, and not by the software, i.e. the X server.

---

[5] Although one could even set 1152 **x** 910 with a 1 MB graphics card memory, for an accelerated X server it would result in a drastic performance loss as it would then have no video memory left over for caching fonts and bitmaps.

The only restriction of some X servers is the limitation of the video signal bandwith to the maximum allowed according to the recommendations in the data sheets supplied by the graphics card manufacturers.

After having entered the **Modes** lines, the configuration of XFree86 is finished. Tell the **xf86config** program that it should store the newly created configuration file under **/etc/X11R6/XF86Config**. Then try to start the X window system with the command **startx**. *startx*

Once the X Window system is running, there are two other tools that may be used to make fine adjustments directly under X11. The advantage is that you can see the effects of changes immediately. The tools are: *Fine tuning directly under X11*

- **vgaset**, with which you can quickly and easily adjust the geometry of the image, and the changed mode entries can be transfered to the **XF86Config** file directly. If you start **vgaset** with the **-d** option and give the clock value of the current video mode, you obtain exact information on the screen refresh rate and horizontal line frequency.[6]

- **xvidtune**, which is a video mode tuner for XFree86. It uses the X server video mode extensions (XFree86-VidModeExtension). It also allows comprehensive and quite comfortable changes of the current settings. With **xvidtune** you can also activate or deactivate power saving for the monitor.

Finally our warning once again: if you experiment with XFree86 or the corresponding optimizing programs, without actually knowing what you are doing, you run the risk of very quickly destroying your monitor as well as your graphics card! *Utmost care when using XF86Config!*

Having read this chapter, you may now understand why we cannot create a configuration file for XFree86. The adjustment of the system to your hardware is and will always be a task for the individual, and a task that can only be automated with some difficulties, if at all.

On the other hand, you are rewarded for your efforts with a freely configured X server extracting optimum performance from your hardware.

---

[6] **vgaset** unfortunately doesn't know the limits of your monitor, so it is up to you to take care not to exceed these limits. For this reason, we decided to no longer supply this tool in the standard distribution. If you want to use it, get it from the second CD-ROM or via ftp. However, if you do use it and a noticable change in the screen image's brilliance occurs, then you should immediately restore the respective value, i.e. the value you altered last.

4.7   The Window Manager FVWM

The FVWM[7] Window manager has established itself as the standard
X11 window manager for Linux. It offers good functionality and con-

*Window
manager*

sumes relatively little memory space. The task of the window manager
is to conduct the graphic elements, for example windows, menus, and
icons, and the events, such as the mouse click or window refresh.

Particular features of the FVWM are the Goodstuff (see Fig. 1.5),

Goodstuff

the launchpad of POWER LINUX and the Pager for the virtual desktop.

The Pager gives you an overall view of the all of your work places,
the virtual screen pages within each work place and indicates which
page you are current viewing. With a mouse click your view leaps from
one page to another. The icon for this bird's eye viewer is located in the
upper left hand side of the launchpad.

Click with the mouse buttons on the desktop background, i.e. not

Popup menus

on a window or window frame and one of three different popup menus
will be displayed. Our default FVWM setting causes the popup menus
to stay open as long as you hold the mouse button down. Try combining
the **CTRL** key with a mouse click to make the menus stay around a little
longer. The mouse buttons open the three main menus as follows:

- left mouse button: the Workplace menu and its submenus, from
  which you can run most programs and applications, change
  configurations, and quit X11,

- middle mouse button: the Window Options menu, in which you
  can call up the most important window operations,

- right mouse button: the window list. The windows listed in this
  menu can take the focus, i.e. become the active window.

Every X11 program uses its own window for its output. An example
is the **xterm** in Fig. 4.5.

Fig. 4.5: A window under Fvwm

---

[7] The acronym FVWM originaly stood for Feeble Virtual Window Manager. But in
the meantime even its author Robert Nation doesn't seem to be sure about it. So,
in the manual page he just named it F(?) Virtual Window Manager.

The window manager adds several elements to the windows. These elements serve for the window operation:

- The title bar states the name of the window. A quick click on the title bar brings the window to the foreground, a double click pushes it into the background, and a click, hold and drag action allows the window to be repositioned.

- The menu button in upper the left hand corner. Clicking on it opens a menu of the most important window operations.

- The quit button in the upper right hand corner. Click here and the program will be ended and the window closed.

- The maximise button in the upper right corner left of the quit button switches the window from its normal to its maximum size and back again.

- The iconify button to the left of the maximise button reduces the window to an icon, but the program keeps on running. Only the output to the window is suspended.

- The frame corners are used to resize the window by clicking and dragging.

- The frame at the sides of the window are used to repostion the window by clicking and dragging it around the workplace.

As already mentioned, the FVWM of POWER LINUX is set up with four virtual pages on the desktop (workplace). You can either change *Virtual desktop* between the pages by clicking on one of the four small windows in the top left hand corner of the launchpad or with the arrow keys. To shift the view with the arrow keys hold down either the **CTRL** or **ALT** key then press one of the arrow keys. The key combinations move the view *Shifting the* of the desktop in the direction of the arrow key. While the **CTRL** moves *visible section* the view page by page the **ALT** moves in smaller increments

Individual windows are displayed in the pager as small rectangles. Moving these rectangles with the middle mouse button shifts the real *Pager functions* windows on the desktop. With the right mouse button you can shift the complete, visible display field within the four virtual screens.

You really should try these functions. When operated properly the pager allows one to work quite efficiently on a very large desktop area.

The active window, that means the window on which the input focus is placed, can be recognized by its colors, which are different *Input focus* from the colors of the non-active windows. POWER LINUX is setup so that the focus always follows the mouse. That means, the active window is always the one under the mouse pointer.

73

Additionally, the "autoraise" function is activated. This function automatically brings the active window to the foreground after about a second. You can also deactivate this function in the desktop submenu.

Autoraise

Also in the desktop submenu you can change the arrangement of the launchpad. Usually it is placed horizontally on the desktop in the upper left hand corner. This is the only arrangement that makes it possible to completely display the launchpad even with a low screen resolution, like for example 640 **x** 480.

*Arrangement
of the launchpad*

If you have set a higher resolution, you can change the launchpad to a vertical arrangement and put it on the right or on the left hand side.

Many functions of the FVWM cannot only be carried out with the mouse, but also directly from the keyboard. The following functions of the FVWM can be activated with the function keys in combination with the **ALT** key:

Key commands

- ALT-F1 calls up the workplace menu (corresponds to the left mouse button),

- ALT-F2 calls up the window option menu, (corresponds to the middle mouse button),

- ALT-F3 calls up the window list, in which the respective windows can be put to the foreground with a mouse click,

- ALT-F4 changes the active window between icon and normal size,

- ALT-F5 moves the active window,

- ALT-F6 changes the size of the active window,

- ALT-F7 changes the focus window to the next window,

- ALT-F8 changes the focus window to the previous window.

We use the the FVWM together with the GNU macro processor m4. It allows the configuration files of the window manager to be structured more clearly, by dividing them into smaller files. POWER LINUX uses following files to configure FVWM:

*GNU m4 macro
processor*

- options; the general behaviour of the Window manager is described here,

- bindings; mouse operations and keyboard commands linked to the actions of the Window manager are determined here,

- menus; this is the template file for all popup menus, which are dynamically created every time the FVWM is started,

- styles; this file determines specific settings for certain applications,

- functions; special functions of the window manager are defined here,

- goodstuff; this file contains all settings for the Goodstuff Launchpad,

- modules; all settings for the external modules of FVWM are entered here.

These configuration files can be found under **/usr/X11R6/lib/** *System wide*
X11/fvwm/system.fvwmrc.<config> as a system wide setting *FVWM*
and under **$HOME/.fvwmrc.<config>** in the user's home direc- *configuration*
tory. Each configuration file can be individually adapted, but this is
recommended for advanced users only.

If syntax errors are introduced or important parts of the configuration are deleted there, the window manager no longer starts at all.

You can also adjust certain settings directly from the desktop menu *Adjusting the*
within the workplace menu, for example: *settings*

- the way the launchpad is to be arranged (above, beneath, on the right or on the left hand side);

- whether the kill button is to be included on the right hand side of every title bar;

- which color setting is to be chosen for the desktop;

- the time delay autoraise leaves before raising a window or whether it should be deactivated;

- the appearance of the desktop background.

The most significant feature of the POWER LINUX FVWM *Dynamic menu*
window manager configuration is its dynamic menu construction. Each *construction*
time FVWM is started, it checks which applications are installed in
the system. Commonly used and otherwise well known programs that
the configuration knows of are sorted into predetermined popup menus
according to category so that the programs are easy to find. All other
programs the configuration finds but does not explicitly know of are also
listed, but in this case are sorted alphabetically in general catalogues.

Applications that existed when the window manager was started,
but are deleted while the window manager is still running, do not cause *Warnings for*
the window manager any problems when you then attempt to start the *missing*
program by selecting it from a menu or clicking on its launchpad icon. *applications*
The window manager simply warns you that the program is not installed
and asks if you would like to reinstall it.

Tools for Daily Work

5.1 Productivity Tools

The reason you have bought a PC will not least lie in the fact that the computer will take over certain tasks or at least make them easier for you. Our Linux therefore provides you with many useful programs, even if at first glance they cannot compete with their Windows equivalents.

Diligent brownies

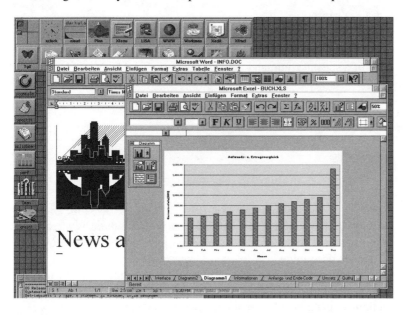

Fig. 5.1: Using Windows programs under Linux with the help of SUN's WABI.

An extremely elegant solution of course, is the use of Windows Application Binary Interface (WABI), the MS Windows emulator from SUN Microsystems, which Caldera has licensed and ported to Linux. It can also be used for POWER LINUX without any problems (Fig. 5.1).

WABI

Combining the
advantages of
both worlds

By using WABI you combine the advantages of both worlds. You can use almost all Windows programs, but underneath a potent Unix system is running. Unix or Linux treats each Windows program as a separate process running within its own protected memory space. When a Windows program crashes under Linux, then only this single process disappears, without affecting the rest of the system. As you may know, this is not always the case with Windows.

WordPerfect
and CorelDraw

Since in the standard POWER LINUX there is, unfortunately, still no WABI included, we turn to the applications which do exist in the system. It is mainly a question of time and experience, until one can do the daily work under Linux in the same way as one might have done under Windows. More and more programs which are common for Windows are now being ported to Linux. We have already mentioned WordPerfect and CorelDraw.

But before you look around for additional program packages, we will show you what's on offer at the house of Linux.

5.1.1 Xman

You have certainly already used the program **man**, to display the manual page of a special command. **xman** is the graphical front end to **man**.

Fig. 5.2: The **xman** program.

Quick help
with Xman

You can put **xman** as an icon (Fig. 5.2) on the desktop. Once the POWER LINUX desktop has started you will see there is already an icon for **xman**. If you click on "manual page", a larger window will be opened describing how to operate **xman**.

Several manual
sections

Under the button "sections" you will find eight different manual sections for the system and a section named "new". Choose one of the sections to get a list of all manual pages included in that section.

Click on the desired page name and the window changes to display this manual page. With the scroll bar, the space bar or the **b** (back) and **f** (forward) keys, you can move around within the document.

Two views

Under the button "options" you can find the entry "show both screens". This divides the window into two areas, one of which is the "overview" of a section's contents and the other is the actual manual page (Fig. 5.3).

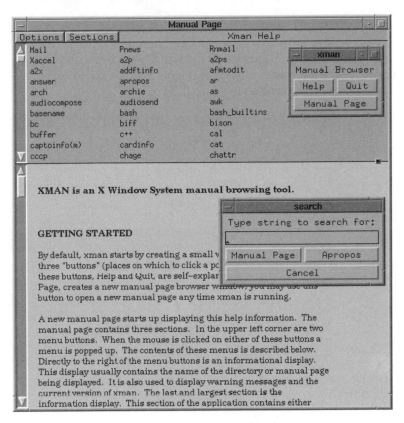

Fig. 5.3: Manual pages under X11.

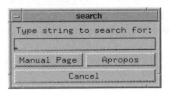

Fig. 5.4: The **xman** search function.

Also under "options" you can find the entry "search", which opens the search menu (Fig. 5.4). From this menu you can search for keywords just within the active manual page, or via "apropos" to find a manual page corresponding to the keyword.

5.1.2 Plan

Filofax and
calendar
all in one

The filofax program **plan** has the "Motif-Look". In the most simple case it can be used just as a calendar. Figure 5.5 shows an annual calendar and an open appointment table.

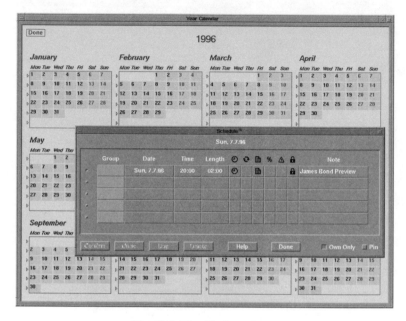

Fig. 5.5: The filofax **plan**.

Closely connected to **plan** is its accompanying daemon **pland**. If you start **plan** and **pland** is not already running, you are advised of this (Fig. 5.6) and you can start the daemon at a later time.

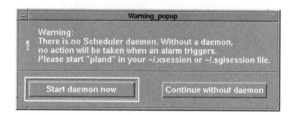

Fig. 5.6: Using **plan** with or without **pland**.

The
daemon
pland

The **pland** daemon supervises your appointments and automatically informs you of forthcoming events or dates. **plan** allows administration of general and private dates in various ways. You can see which configuration files **plan** uses by having a look at its manual page.

5.1.3 Tree Browser

The tree browser **tb** by Rudolf Koenig is an extremely useful tool to graphically find one's way in the file system or to quickly find certain information in the directory tree (Fig. 5.7).

Clear
directory
trees

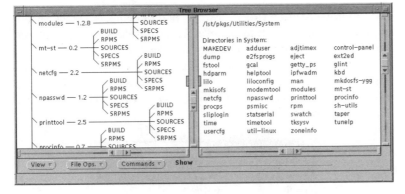

Fig. 5.7: The file system browser **tb**.

You have the option of either opening each directory's subtree by hand or to let them be automatically recursively opened. The file trees created thereby can be stored as images in PostScript files (Menu: "commands", "write PS").

Under the entry "more" in the "view" menu you can find, somewhat hidden, the useful function "hide specified" (Fig. 5.8).

The output of **tb**, by the way, can be optimized easily by hand. While the program always tries to optimize the file trees display vertically, you can also optimize the file tree display horizontally. This goes as follows: while pressing the **SHIFT** key, click with the left mouse button on the centre of the directory; hold the button and drag the centre. Just have a try.

Optimizing
outputs
by hand

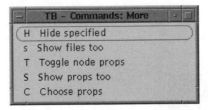

Fig. 5.8: The More menu of **tb**.

Apart from its function of displaying file trees **tb**, can also be used as a file manager. You can move, copy or delete directories or files by clicking on them. A double click with the mouse on single files in the

File manager
included

81

right-hand window causes these to be displayed in a special browser window.

5.1.4 Performance Meter

Displaying the
system load

The performance meter **perf**, also by Rudolf Koenig, is a practical tool for displaying the system load. Several system values can be displayed in different sub-windows simultaneously (Fig. 5.9).

The most interesting values are probably the processor capacity utilization ("cpu"), which states the present capacity utilization of the processor, as well as the system load ("load"), which displays the total load on the system.

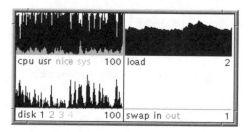

Fig. 5.9: The performance meter **perf**.

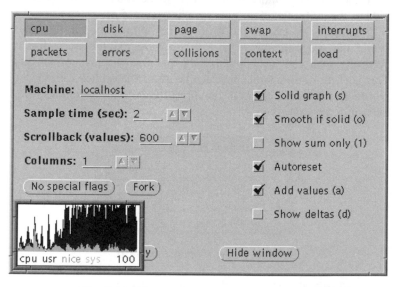

Fig. 5.10: The configuration menu of **perf**.

With the left mouse button you can move the display area of every sub-window, to retrieve values which have disappeared off the left-hand side.

The comprehensive configuration options of **perf** are in a special window (Fig. 5.10), which is opened with the right mouse button. To activate your changes click the "apply" button.

The performance meter requires the **rstatd** daemon to be running. This daemon is activated automatically when your Linux system starts. If it doesn't happen to be running, though, **perf** will give you a corresponding warning and you can start **rstatd** later.

The daemon rstatd

5.1.5 Xfm

The file and application manager **xfm** (Fig. 5.11) offers all the functions which one usually expects from a file manager. You can move within the filesystem, copy, delete or move files and start programs with a mouse click.

File and program manager all in one

If the contents of the depicted directories changes, it will be updated automatically at certain intervals. You can choose between a tree or detailed depiction.

The application manager makes it possible to administer programs or files by arranging them in groups. It is also possible to associate a mouse click on files or programs with particular actions. For example, your favourite editor can be started when you click on a text file.

Applications arranged in groups

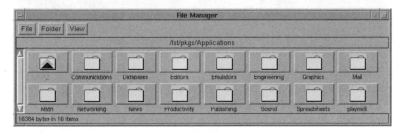

Fig. 5.11: The file manager **xfm**.

A special feature of **xfm** is that it can also be configured so that it automatically mounts the respective file systems when changing to certain directories, and unmounts them again when leaving the directory. If you click for example on **cdrom** in the directory **/mnt**, then **xfm** will try to mount the currently inserted CD-ROM and then display its contents.

Automatic mounting for specific directories

5.2   Graphic Tools

Of course, working with a graphical interface would only be half as nice if there were no tools and programs with which to create and adapt graphical elements or colored icons. For this purpose too, Linux offers a number of interesting programs.

5.2.1   xv

Supporting various graphic formats

The graphic tool **xv** by John Bradley (Fig. 5.12) is an excellent tool for working on or converting graphics of various formats.

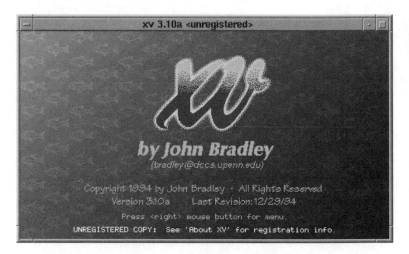

Fig. 5.12: The graphics program **xv**.

The size and proportions of images can be changed, hues can be adapted and pictures can be put in the X11 background (Fig. 5.13).

Color editor

The color editor (Fig. 5.14) is endowed with a wide range of functions. **xv** can work on pictures with hues up to 24 bit and can also be used as a file system browser.

The ability to simultaneously display all graphics included in a directory in one window as Thumbnails is extremely practical. To do

Icon Manager

this choose the entry "update icons" in the menu "Misc Commands" of the "Visual Schnauzer".

xv is shareware

xv is shareware and should be registered with the author if you use the program often. There are different gradings, which differentiate between private and commercial use. In any case **xv** is worth the money.

An alternative to **xv** are the tools **xli** (also known as **xload-image**) or the comprehensive ImageMagick graphics package. Both are contained in POWER LINUX .

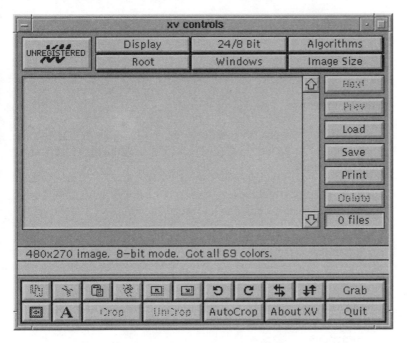

Fig. 5.13: The main menu of **xv**.

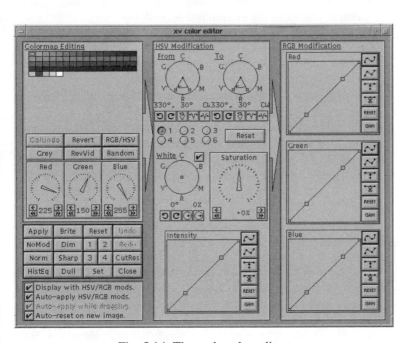

Fig. 5.14: The **xv**'s color editor.

5.2.2 xpaint

*Draw program
with many colors*

The graphics program **xpaint** (Fig. 5.15) provides you with all the common functions of a painting program and is good for working with colors. Amongst other things, it makes it possible to work on the following formats:

- TIFF (tag image file format) – an easily exchangable format, common on many platforms, which is used as **xpaint**'s standard format;

- GIF (graphics interchange format) – the favourite graphic format in the internet, which also has broad support;

- PPM (portable pixmap) – the format used by the graphic package PBMplus, which allows conversion into many other formats;

- XBM (X11 bitmap) – mono color bitmaps as used under X11;

- XPM (X11 pixmap) – pixmaps of multiple colors stored in the ASCII format, which therefore can easily be included into programs;

- XWD – the output format of **xwd** (xwindump), with which screen dumps can be stored as graphics under X11.

Xpaint tools menu

Once **xpaint** has been started from the launchpad, the **xpaint** tools menu appears. The most important drawing functions can be operated by clicking on their respective symbols.

Canvas

To make a new image, create a canvas with "new canvas" from the "file" menu. To load an existing graphics file use "open".

*Xpaint main
window*

After either of these steps, the main window of **xpaint** is opened. You can open several of these main windows and each uses its own colors palette.

The "help" button opens a very detailed and complete online help, which allows quick access via a special topic menu. The "image" button starts the "fat bits" editor, used for the enlargement of sections. This editor can depict a section of a picture at various zoom levels. In this editor all the graphical operations can be used just as in the main canvas window.

The fat bits editor

*Any enlarge-
ment at all*

The visible areas of the main canvas itself can also be changed with the function "change zoom". When making enlargements from factor 1 upwards, a grid can be inserted between the single pixels, so that they can be worked on very precisely.

Color wheel

Individual colors can easily be chosen from the color wheel. With the "lookup" function, hues can be chosen directly from the image.

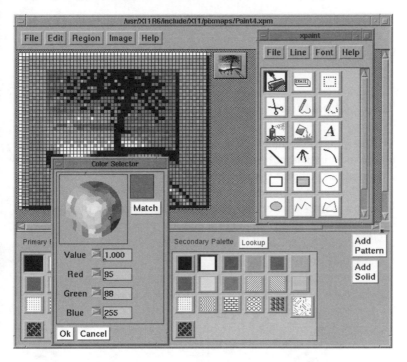

Fig. 5.15: The painting and drawing program **xpaint**.

xpaint offers a variety of yet further useful functions. In the clipboard, picture sections or whole images can be saved. The font browser allows a practical preview and selection of all installed and available X11 fonts. The eraser not only deletes pixels, but also restores the original background. So, if you made additions i.e. wrote or painted on the picture, the eraser will only delete the additional changes to the desired extent, and not the original background.

Font browser
Intelligent eraser

5.3 Publishing

One of the most important tasks of PCs nowadays will surely be the production and layout of documents and correspondence. Since the heyday of the good old typewriter now belongs to the distant past, one catches oneself frequently spending too much of one's time with lavishly jazzing up the mostly quickly written texts with colors, pictures, and special layout.

Documents
of all kinds

This, of course, is an essential strength of modern PCs in comparison to the typewriter and therefore we want to introduce you to some of the tools offered by Linux.

*Practice makes
perfect*

With some practice and experience you will be able to solve most publishing problems under Linux. It may take some time to get accustomed to the operation.

5.3.1 Ghostscript

*Powerful page des-
cription language*

PostScript is a common file format[1] under Unix. Maybe it is even one of the most important formats of all when it comes to the professional layout of text, graphics and documents.

*Perfect printing
on low cost printers
as well*

A PostScript document can be printed without changes on a cheap low cost printer as well as on a wickedly expensive Linotype print record machine, always as the best possible printing quality.

Red   Green **Blue**   Yellow Pink   Cyan   'White'
Fig. 5.16: A small PostScript file with a great effect.

---

[1] to be more exact, PostScript is much more than just a file format, it is a very powerful page description language. You will believe this when you have seen a PostScript file, consisting of few lines only, keeping the PostScript printer "busy" for several minutes, and drawing a giant raytraced picture from it.

As impressive as the advantages of PostScript may be, not every one of us has a PostScript printer to call his or her own for actually printing PostScript documents. To cure this problem one can easily take remedial action under Linux.

Namely, the program ghostscript (**gs**). Ghostscript is a complete PostScript interpreter; that means it can read PostScript files and execute the instructions they contain. The output which results from that can either be displayed under X11 via the frontend **ghostview** or be sent to almost any printer at hand.

PostScript interpreter

This works independently of which printer you use. It just has to be a graphics printer supported by Ghostscript. Using **gs** even a simple 9 pin dot matrix printer can print PostScript documents in astonishingly high quality.

Just needs a graphics printer

Normally you won't run **gs** directly, but use it in the background or as part of a filter. If, for example, the lpr-NG printing package is configured for your system and you print a PostScript file with the command **lpr**, the printing system passes the file on to a printing filter which recognizes from the characteristics of the file that it is a PostScript file. Then it calls up **gs** to convert the file to a bitimage format, which can be printed out by the printer and returns these data to the printing system. The printing system then sends these data to the printer.

Lpr-NG printing system

Bitimage data for the printer

Many programs also indirectly use **gs** when they have to read in PostScript files. For example, if you use **xv** for displaying a PostScript file, you will notice that **xv** doesn't do everything itself, but rather uses **gs** for the transformation to displayable graphics data.

Moving spirit, which stays in the background

The various output devices (Devices), for example X11 or printers, that are supported by your version of **gs** can be displayed by entering the command:

Output devices

```
gs -help
```

This list corresponds exactly to the printer types that LISA offered for selection during the installation. If you run **gs** without options, then after initializing, the program will give you a command input prompt (**GS>**) and a white output window is opened.

Supported printers

Now you can load a PostScript document or directly type in PostScript commands. If this results in valid output, this is then displayed in the output window. You can find example documents in PostScript and all control data sets and configuration files for **gs** in the directory **/usr/lib/ghostscript**.

Commands for gs

As already indicated in the footnote, PostScript is not only a simple file format, that can easily be transferred to the various platforms, but it is at the same time a complete programming language. There are hackers of the "old school" who write their PostScript documents by hand or don't just use PostScript for documents.

Programming with PostScript

*Help program
in PostScript*

You should really cast an eye over a Postscript file just once. It only consists of ASCII characters and can be displayed with **less**. Also, in the **gs** home directory **/usr/lib/ghostscript** you can find a number of PostScript files. Only the README file is a plain text file and the PostScript files are not documents. They are in fact ancilliary programs programmed in PostScript and therefore require **gs** in order to run. The PostScript file **ps2ascii.ps** serves the purpose of converting PostScript documents into plain ASCII text.

ps2ascii

Figure 5.16 shows the PostScript page **colorcir.ps**, which is located in the directory **/usr/lib/ghostscript/examples**. The size of **colorcir.ps** is just 1800 Bytes. Watch the construction process of this graphic when it is displayed with **ghostview** or **xdvi** and you will notice that an iteration takes place.

5.3.2 Ghostview

Rather than using **gs** you can view the output of PostScript files more easily with the frontend **ghostview** (Fig. 5.17).

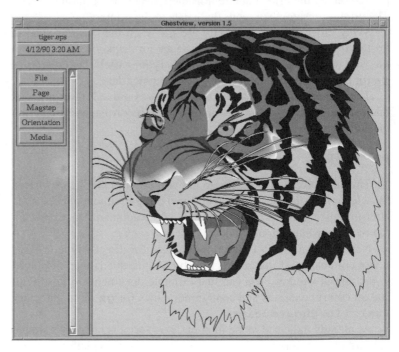

Fig. 5.17: The Ghostscript frontend **ghostview**.

Paper sizes

With **ghostview** you can also determine paper sizes and orientation (portrait or landscape) and adjust the enlargement in several steps.

The ablilty to directly choose individual pages in larger documents or to mark special pages for working on them is very convenient. Individual pages can be printed as well.

Directly choosing special pages

5.3.3 LaTeX

The publishing system TeX/LaTeX is astonishing in many ways. LaTeX is very flexible and is available for almost every operating system. As only the plain ASCII text is used for LaTeX documents, these are transportable wherever you like. Of course the final output is not restricted to plain text.

LaTeX documents are readable

Even when one is under way with an old XT or 286er laptop with a text only display one can still prepare LaTeX documents using any available text editor. Later the LaTeX documents can be processed with any computer on which the TeX/LaTeX system is installed and have the output printed in high quality.

High quality print is one of the specialities of this program package. LaTeX documents can quickly and easily be converted to every other major format. Aside from TeX's own DVI (Device Independent) format, HTML, PostScript or special image data, e.g. for Hewlett Packard printers, can be created at the push of a button.

High print quality

Thanks to this variety of formats one is not dependent on a particular output device or a printer driver. Once again the advantages of Linux can be seen clearly, as it comes with WWW browsers for viewing HTML and **ghostview** for working with PostScript files.

Flexible formats

As is so often the case, there is a small price to pay for all these features and power. When working with LaTeX the first time you may feel like you are going back in time to when the computer era was still in its infancy.

The WYSIWYG (What you see is what you get) will be probably replaced by "What you want is what you might get". To be more precise, this means that a LaTeX document which, as we already mentioned, is a pure ASCII text file consisting of your text and the layout control structures that you include, must first of all be compiled by TeX before the pleasing result can be viewed.

Documents must be replaced first

That means you first enter the control structures to specify what you want and LaTeX tries to resolve all control structures while compiling the source document. As can one might imagine the result sometimes differs slightly from what was actually intented. On the other hand LaTeX's powerful macros correctly carry out many complex tasks with very little effort from yourself.

Advantages and disadvantages of compiling

LaTeX always creates DVI files first, which are independent of the final output device. These files can either be displayed with the program

Device independent

xdvi (Fig. 5.18) or be converted into the desired final format with a program such as **dvips** into the PostScript format.

The combination of LaTeX, **xdvi** multiple X11 windows and multitasking gives you "What you see is what you wrote a few seconds ago". You will appreciate the benefits of this method if you have ever had to wait for your word processor to finish formating your document before you can continue typing.

The layout is done by LaTeX

LaTeX makes the layout and all formatting completely by itself. You just have to decide for a certain layout style, like for example a book or a letter, and insert control structures to mark where chapters, lists, or tables etc. begin and end.

Plenty of documentation

LaTeX takes over everything else. Only if you are not content with the output will you need to do additional work on the document. If you want to occupy yourself more intensively with LaTeX, you can find plenty of documentation starting in the directory **/usr/TeX/doc**.

Figure 5.18 shows the "Installation and Maintenance Guide" for teTeX, a very good and widespread LaTeX compendium by Thomas Esser, which we use for the POWER LINUX . This figure also shows the program **xdvi** in action.

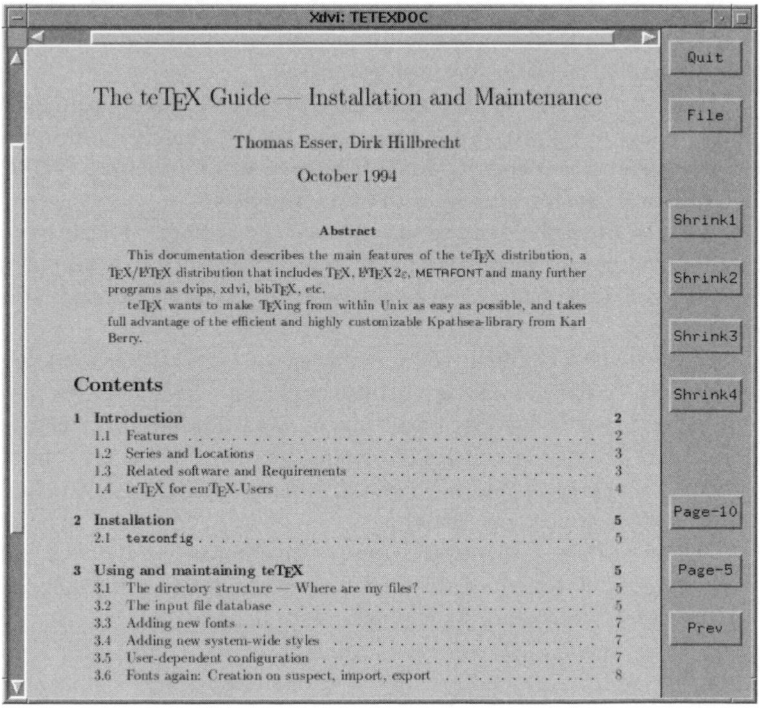

Fig. 5.18: The dvi viewer **xdvi**.

In passing we'll give you a hint: do not give up too fast. In the past we ourselves have chosen to use a "typical word processing system". Once we decided to write this book completely for LaTeX, a certain training period was necessary. In the meanwhile however, we are sure that if we had to write a book again from scratch we wouldn't do it with any other text processing system or word processor.

LaTeX often can be the first choice

As soon as you have had your first feeling of success with LaTeX you will know what we mean.

5.3.4 Lyx

With the relatively new program **lyx**, handling LaTeX can be greatly simplified. **lyx** in principle, is a frontend for LaTeX. **lyx** uses the Xforms library, a GUI[2] toolkit for X11. It extends LaTeX by providing the missing WYSIWYG feature (Fig. 5.19) and is therefore called a "High Level Word Processor" by its authors.

WYSIWYG for LaTeX

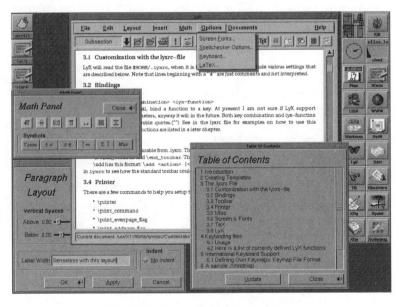

Fig. 5.19: The LaTeX frontend **lyx**.

In practice this means that **lyx** continually provides an image of the document. In this image you can edit in the same way as in any other word processor. You no longer have to worry about the LaTeX control structures as **lyx** itself creates the LaTeX source document.

Document source text remains hidden

---

[2] graphical user interface

So, you can prepare the source document as usual by hand or just let **lyx** do it all for you. If you so desire, all LaTeX details remain hidden by **lyx**.

Early beta version

Even though today **lyx** is only available in a very early version (pre 0.10.7), it makes a promising impression nevertheless, and already runs stably enough. As there will probably be some changes to **lyx** in the time to come and as good online documentation exists, we will refrain from an overly detailed description at this point.

All LaTeX features are accessible

In essence, **lyx** gives you all the features of LaTeX, such as easily creating mathematical formulae, tables, enumerations, and text attributes in menus. You are able to use them directly in the visible document. A particular layout can be chosen, the formatting can be adapted individually or the document can be checked for spelling.

5.3.5 Tgif

Hypertext extensions

The program **tgif** (Fig. 5.20) is an object orientated drawing program with hypertext extensions, which can create and work on a variety of file formats. It can be used in two completely different operating modes:

- as a interactive drawing and constructing program, or

- as a filter for the print output, whereby the program just works in the background.

Interactive mode

In the interactive mode **tgif** can either be called up directly with an object file or with a URL,[3] which points to a file available via the network.

Filter mode

In the filter mode **tgif** converts object files to PostScript, Encapsulated PostScript (EPS) for including in LaTeX documents or sends them directly to the printing system.

Unfortunately, not all formats are available in the filter mode. The formats X11 bitmap, X11 pixmap, GIF or color PostScript can only be created in the interactive mode.

Running tgif with object files

If you want to use **tgif** in the interactive mode, you can either start it from the launchpad or start it up with an object file (*.obj) as argument from the shell. A working sheet in US-letter format will appear.

Metric grid

Choose the option "metric grid" from the menu "layout" and you will get a grid with centimeter spacing. With the functions "portrait" and "landscape" in the "layout" menu you can choose between a horizontal or vertical work sheet.

---

[3] Uniform Resource Locator, a link to a FTP or HTTP server, such as http://www.ncsa.uiuc.edu/General/Internet/WWW/HTMLPrimer.html for example.

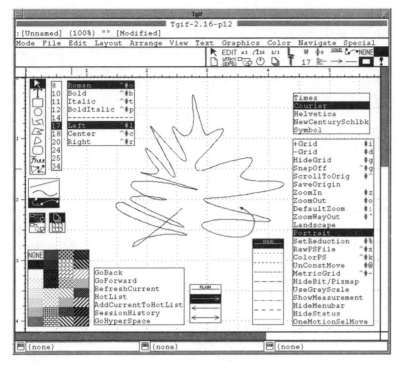

Fig. 5.20: The program **tgif**.

To operate **tgif** you need a three button mouse.[4] A desription of the function which would be activated by pressing the mouse buttons is displayed in the message bar above the lower edge of the window.

Three button mouse necessary

It is possible to drag certain menus, once they have been opened, from the upper menu strip and to drop them onto the desired place on the X11 interface, for getting faster access to frequently used menu items. This is especially practical for the mode menu, from which one can select the drawing modes.

Movable menus

Note that you have to call up the individual functions from these menus with the middle mouse button. With the right mouse button, the menu disappears again and with the left mouse button you can move it to another position.

Functions of the mouse buttons

Take the time to get a general idea of the various and often powerful functions which are contained in the menus. The most important basic settings can be seen at the upper edge, below the main menu labels.

Basic settings are displayed

These settings can be changed either via the respective menu items or by directly clicking on them. When the second method is chosen,

---

[4] If you only have a two button mouse, then affirm the option "emulate 3 buttons" for the X server, in order to be able to simulate the middle button by pressing both mouse buttons simultaneously.

either an input field is opened or you can increase the values with the left mouse button or decrease them with the right one.

A very practical function is hidden in the "file" menu under the entries "BrowseXBitmap" or "BrowseXPixmap"; thereby the bitmap or pixmap files are sought in the current working directory. Each bitmap or pixmap found is then automatically inserted into the current document. These pixmap or bitmap graphics can then be edited as individual objects. Best try this function in the directory **/usr/X11R6/include/ X11/pixmaps**.

Bitmap and pixmap browser

For each function there are also shortcuts, stated after the menu items. These allow faster and more efficient work.

If, for example, you copy an object, previously marked with **CTRL-y** (Yank), with **CTRL-d** (Duplicate) and place it a certain distance from the original, all further duplicates, which you create with **CTRL-d** are automatically placed the same distance from the previous duplicate.

Convenient shortcuts

The **tgif** program offers further features, which do not stand out at first glance. It supports a "hyperspace mode", which can be activated with the function "GoHyperspace" from the "navigate" menu. The hyperspace mode is activated automatically, if **tgif** is started with an URL as argument. In the hyperspace mode certain objects are treated as hot links. If the mouse pointer is placed on such a hot link object, it changes to the figure of a hand to indicate the fact that clicking on this object will cause a certain action.

Hyperspace mode

Hot link objects

To transform an object into a hot link object, one must provide it with one of the following attributes: "TELEPORT", "LAUNCH APPLICATIONS" or "INTERNAL COMMANDS". With these you can skip to other objects, which may also be located on another page, start certain applications, or to run internal commands.

Automatically starting applications

Details on these mechanisms can be found in the manual page for **tgif**.

5.3.6 Xfig

On first glance, the program **xfig** (Fig. 5.21) appears quite similar to **tgif**, but it lays more emphasis on drawing and construction. It does not offer any hypertext functions, but instead it can handle LaTeX graphics very well.

Drawings and LaTeX graphics

xfig too provides a grid with inch units by default. The command line option **-me** may be applied if you want to start it in metric mode. It is also recommended that the option **-but_ 3** is used to provide the menu icons with a third column on the left hand edge. This has the effect that the operation window gains some vertical space, and the organisa-

Important startup option

tion of the icons is clearer. If you start **xfig** from the launchpad, these options will already be set.

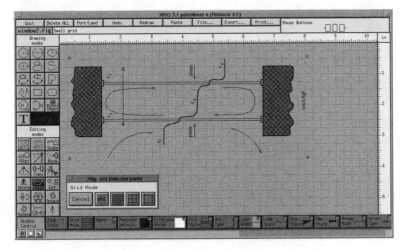

Fig. 5.21: The layout program **xfig**.

As with **tgif**, **xfig** also displays the actions which can be acti- *Mouse actions* vated with the mouse buttons. *and icons*

The icon line at the very bottom of the operation window is called the indicator panel, in which further icons are shown depending on the drawing function chosen. With these you can initiate actions corresponding to the drawing function.

5.3.7 XEmacs

Speaking briefly about Emacs is surely as difficult as explaining Emacs *Emacs, the king* in full. So, we elegantly dodge this by reassuring you that Emacs is the *of the editors* most fantastic editor and that we decided, for this POWER LINUX, to do without it in favour of **xemacs** (Fig. 5.22).

xemacs strives to deliver all the benefits of Emacs combined with *The two emacs are* user friendly colorful icons and menus. Both versions are coming closer *merging again* to each other at the moment and some time in the near future they will be once again fused into a single version.

Please do not pass up the opportunity of starting **xemacs** and click- *Documentation for* ing through all the menus. If you find it pleasing, then buy one of the *Emacs is a rich and* heavy tomes on Emacs and make your diploma in "Emacs-ology". *heavy load*

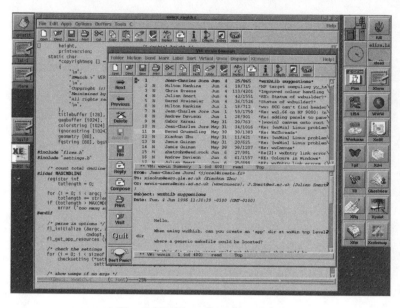

Fig. 5.22: The editor **xemacs**.

5.4   Internet Tools

X11 frontends

Now let's leave the publishing tools theme and turn to the X11 programs that provide you with the classic internet information services under the X window system in a simple and clear way.

5.4.1   Xftp

File Transfer Protocol

One of the most commonly used internet services is FTP.[5] FTP facilitates the transfer of files from other computers on the net, called FTP servers, to your computer or to put data from your own computer onto the FTP server. These tranfers are known as downloading and uploading respectively.

Frontend for ftp

Of course you can just do this on the command line too, with the program **ftp**. It is easier, though, to use the X11 frontend **xftp** for this purpose (Fig. 5.23).

External viewer

xftp allows target and source directories, choosing files, adjusting transfer modes and setting connections to the local or to other computers to be set easily. You also have the opportunity of just having a look at the files, instead of transferring them to your local file system. This works not only with text files, but also with graphics, for example.

---

[5] File transfer protocol.

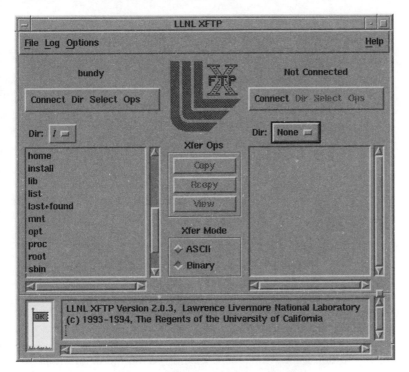

Fig. 5.23: The ftp frontend **xftp**.

In the "options" menu, under "viewer preferences" you can determine which external viewer, such as **xv**, should be called upon for this purpose.

If you first want to get some practice with **xftp** then you should also set your local computer as the target computer (on the right hand side). That means the connection will be set from your computer to your computer and all functions of **xftp** will still be available. *Connect to Localhost*

Note that you have to activate the binary transport mode, when transferring programs or image data. This is also the case with **ftp**. Only for plain ASCII and text files, is it sufficient to use the quicker ASCII mode. *Binary Mode*

5.4.2 Xarchie

For the text based information system **archie** there is also the corresponding frontend **xarchie** for X11 (Fig. 5.24). The archie internet information system gives you information on where to get particular files or programs per FTP. Your archie client instructs an archie server to search through databases containing information on the large part of the files available on the Internet. *Frontend to the archie information service*

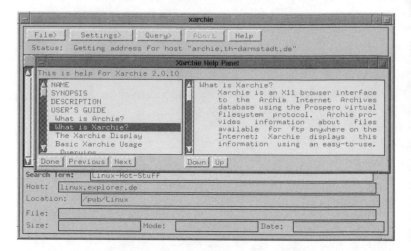

Fig. 5.24: The archie frontend **xarchie**.

*The right source
for every situation*

For the search you can either choose a computer with an archie
server or the desired FTP archives. **xarchie** comes with a list of the
most important archie servers, from which you only have to choose a
server near to you.

Search filters

If you don't known the name of the specific file or files that you
want then you can apply general search filters. You can also search for
regular expressions or for parts of a word. **xarchie** then returns the
URLs for each file found as a result of the search.

*WWW search
machines*

It is necessary, of course, to have Internet access, if you want to
search with archie. As there is such an enormous amount of data available in the Internet, it is almost a must to use information services like
archie. As an alternative you can of course also query one of the many
WWW search engines via a Web browser.

5.4.3 Arena

*Copyright for
Web browsers*

A number of Web browsers are available for Linux. But for copyright
reasons only the **arena** Web browser (Fig. 5.25) can be distributed
on CD-ROM, and then only as a binary version, that is, without source
code.

*Free from
the Internet*

But if you have access to the Internet then you will also be able to
download the other Web browsers for private use. The favourites are
Netscape (see sect. 5.4.4) and Mosaic.

*ASCII based
browser Lynx*

There is even a purely ASCII based browser named **lynx** which
can be used without, X11. You can find these browsers on nearly
every Linux mirror site, like for example ftp://uni-erlangen.de:/pub/
Linux/MIRROR.sunsite/system/Network/info-systems.

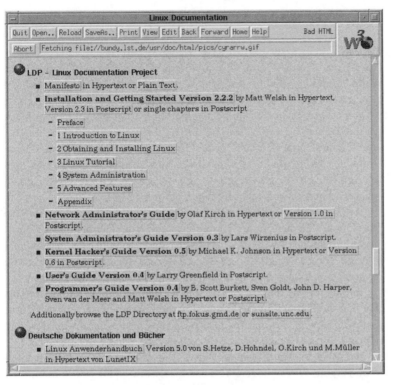

Fig. 5.25: The Web browser **arena**.

A large part of the Linux and system documentation is meanwhile available in hyper-text markup language (HTML), the file format for Web pages. If you choose the top item from the window manager "workplace" menu, the system help item, then you will get a selection of numerous important WWW pages on the system.

HTML Documentation

A text element, highlighted by another color is a hyperlink. Clicking on a hyperlink causes the information it points to to be displayed. A hyperlink may point to another part of the text or to another page. If you click on the icon "home", the view reverts to the first page. The "back" icon switchs the view to the previously viewed page.

Hyperlinks for good cross-references

If you have already made a connection to the internet, you can feverishly hurl yourself into the "Web surfing mania" and choose a new page on the WWW server with the "open" button. As dozens of new WWW servers are connected to the grid every day, we will just recommend beginning with our own Web server **www.1st.de**.

Been surfing today?

5.4.4 Netscape

The favourite
browser

The WWW browser **Netscape Navigator** (Fig. 5.26) is surely one of the favourite and most often used browsers within the Unix world. Thanks to this browser the Netscape company has experienced an almost meteoric rise[6] and has been market leader for a long time. New browsers are becomming available all the time and each has it pros and cons.

Java

Of course, that is all the better for the user – after all competition stimulates the market and innovation. **Netscape Navigator** was the first browser to also suppport Java, the new platform independent object orientated programming language from SUN.

Animated
graphics

At the moment Java is mainly used for animated graphics in Web pages, but in the near future it may save you from having to buy expensive application software in many cases. With the help of a Java capable browser you can load the newest versions of Java programs from the internet. You then just have to pay for the time you use the programs.

Software directly
from the net

In the end this may be much cheaper than buying special programs that one would seldom use. The hardware resources of your computer are saved as well, because the Java based software downloaded from the network will not be stored locally on your hard disk.

One browser
for all tasks

Netscape Navigator shows that a browser is not just limited to displaying WWW pages. You can also work on all your e-mail, read news or administer your email addresses. The only thing missing is an integrated word processor, but they may already be working on that.

Crossed ribbon

If you happened to notice the crossed ribbon, the "blue ribbon", (which unfortunately is not completely visible) in the figure below, then look out for it appearing again. It has been chosen by internet users as the symbol for freedom of speech, opinion, and data, due to the recent moves toward radical censorship regulations for the internet thoughout by government agencies.

Black sheep
amongst the
internet users

It is unfortunately true that there are black sheep amongst the approximately 30 to 40 million internet users, who have brought the internet bad press by uploading pornography, or as a bizzare example uploading instructions found in the local library on how to build a bomb. In the past the internet community has kept itself in check successfully.

As is to be expected this self control has come under strain due to the explosive growth of the internet. No pun intended. Discussions on this topic have been known to be full of ironies. We nevertheless hope

---

[6] Netscape went onto the stock market very early and at the beginning it was almost the only company, with which one could invest in internet technology. Netscape thus experienced incredible capital gains till the end of 1995. Since 1996, though, this tendency has been clearly slowed down, so that it unfortunately is too late now to invest in Netscape.

that self control will also be possible in the future without over zealous intrusions from officialdom.

We can give the following tip to those of you who don't yet have access to the Internet, the price of Caldera Network Desktop includes a Netscape Navigator license. Your Internet service provider will in most cases only give you a sampler version of a Web browser.

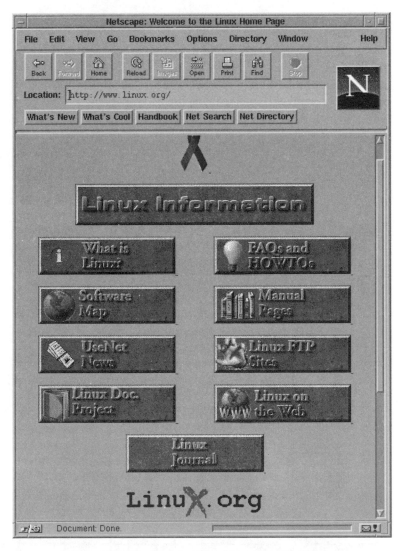

Fig. 5.26: The Web browser Netscape Navigator

5.5   Games and Pastimes

The fact that games are very popular amongst the numerous internet
freaks and programmers is obvious from the wide selection of games
and utilities to pass the time available for Linux. From the selection we
picked out a few interesting programs.

5.5.1   GNU Chess

*Frontend to
gnuchess*

The program **xboard** is the X11 frontend to the demanding GNU chess
program **gnuchess**. You can play **gnuchess** directly on the console,
but then it is purely text oriented. The use of **xboard** under X11 (Fig.
5.27) makes playing chess much more comfortable.

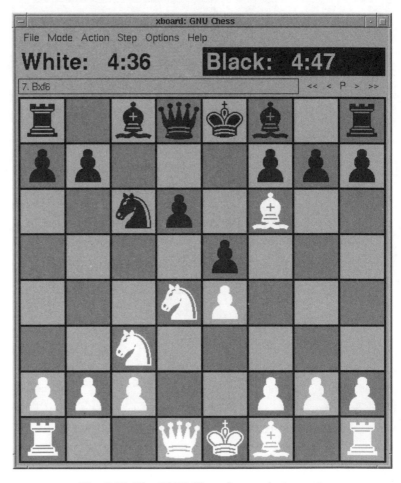

Fig. 5.27: The GNU Chess frontend **xboard**.

xboard displays a 2D chessboard upon which the playing pieces can be moved with the mouse. **xboard** has nothing to do with the moves, these are calculated in the background, by **gnuchess**.

Chessboard and game engine are separate

Even experienced chess players will be surprised by the game's skill level. We have watched good players, who believed they had found an easy opponent in **gnuchess**, but who were checkmated within surprisingly few moves. It will surely be of interest to beginners that there is the possibility of getting a hint ("hint") for the next move. You can also display the strategy that **gnuchess** calculates and considers.

High skill game level

You can store any game you want, go back to a certain move or create your own situations. It is also possible to let the computer play against itself. Note however that **gnuchess** already needs relatively large amounts of storage space in the one-player mode.

A lot of storage space needed

5.5.2 Xanim

The animation player **xanim** can play a number of different image and animation files:

Animation formats

- FLI animations,

- FLC animations,

- IFF animations,

- GIF graphics, which can also be animated via a control data set,

- DL animation files,

- Amiga PFX animation files,

- Utah Raster Toolkit RLE graphics and animations,

- Quicktime animations,

- MPEG animations,

- WAV audio data.

A special feature of **xamin** is the combination of various formats. Figure 5.28 shows a static image from an example animation with the control panel of **xanim**.

With options you can influence the behaviour of **xanim** to a certain degree. It is also possible to enlarge sections with the mouse, while an animation is running.

Section enlargement

Audio support though, is only possible when the sound driver is correctly initialized. You can either include the sound support with your

Sound support

custom system kernel or load it as a kernel module. While the kernel module approach takes up memory only when the sound driver is needed, the compiled in sound driver has the advantage that it can be adapted more individually.

Fig. 5.28: The animation player **xanim**.

Sound driver via
kernel module

The sound driver in POWER LINUX , which is loadable as a kernel module, supports the main standard sound cards, which work with the common default settings. To adapt the sound driver more precisely, we recommend that you read the sound and the sound playing HOWTOs.

5.5.3 Xearth

Extra lessons
in geography

For everyone who missed the geography lessons in school, the program **xearth** offers good supplementary lessons. As a background image for X11, it shows the Earth in at high resolution with the largest cities indicated (5.29).

Viewing the Earth
from the Sun

The angle of vision on the Earth is determined by the longitude currently sunlit.[7] You view the Earth from the direction of the Sun. The twilight zones are given a shadowed appearance.

Updating in 5
minutes interval

Per default the image of the Earth is updated every 5 minutes. The interval can be adjusted to the second via the **-wait** parameter. Do not choose an interval that is too short, because it always takes some time to calculate the position of the Earth. The option **-once** turns off the rotation completely and you just get a motionless background image.

Latitude and
longitude

If you don't want a depiction of the lightest point, but another one, you can get it by stating the degree of longitude and latitude with the help of the **-pos** option.

Alternative views

The marking of cities can be turned off with the option **-nomarker** and the constellations that surround the Earth can be faded out with

---

[7] Provided that the hardware clock of your computer is set to Greenwich Mean-time (GMT), as is right and proper for a Linux computer.

-notars. The command line option **-mag** makes it possible to magnify the Earth; and with **-grid**, the degrees of longitude and latitude can be displayed in addition.

Fig. 5.29: The Earth as background image with **xearth**.

The depiction of **xearth** can also be influenced with a number of further options. For these you can either call up the manual page for **xearth** or get the options with **xearth --help**.

5.5.4 Xfractint

The fractal generator **xfractint** was ported from the DOS program of the same name **fractint** to Linux (Fig. 5.30). In addition to the output window, in which the fractals are constructed, **xfractint** uses a second window for changing the options.

Generate fractals

There is also an online help available with cross references to every command. The help texts though, remain unchanged from the DOS version and all the descriptions on the different graphics modes and drivers are of no importance under Linux.

*Graphics drivers
are not necessary
under X11*

If you mark an area in the output window with the mouse, it will be zoomed, that means, the marked area is enlarged. This works until you reach the limits of the maximum iteration depth or the integer precision of the calculation.

Zooming a section

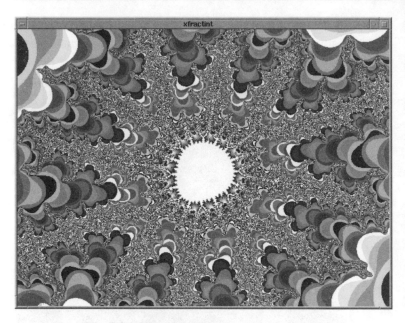

Fig. 5.30: The fractal program **xfractint**.

*Images in
several stages*

Fractal functions

xfractint builds up the image in several stages, which gives a quick overview of the developing image. In the menu "basic option" this can be reduced to a single stage by setting "passes = 1".

In the menu "fractal type" you can choose from more than 50 different fractal parameters and functions - enough to while away a whole evening. You can store your pieces of art at any time as GIF graphics, or store or load the picture parameters only.

Julia parameter

With the space key you can switch to the Julia parameter or display these in reduced size in the lower right hand corner of the output window at any time. A 3D mode can also be activated for each fractal.

Mxp

If you found **xfractint** pleasurable, then you should really try the fractal program **mxp** too. Though **mxp** hasn't the comprehensive functions of **xfractint**, it is much more easy to operate. We'll therefore refrain from a further description.

5.5.5 Xmine

A well-known addictive drug is the minesweeper game, which you will be familiar with from Windows. Under Linux it is called **xmine** or **xdemineur**. See Fig. 5.31.

*Attention: danger
of becoming
addicted!*

The aim of the game is to discover by deduction all mines which are hidden on the board, without clicking on them. The first click is carried out "blind", then you are always shown the number of mines bordering on a field. If no mines are bordering on a field, the program uncovers the safe area until it finds further mines.

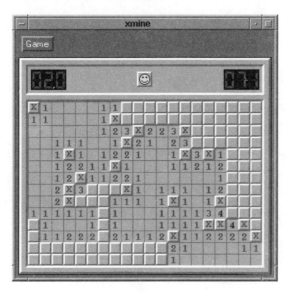

Fig. 5.31: The minesweeper **xmine**.

Of course it's not just the aim not to step on a mine, it is more impor-tant to clear the board as quickly as possible. The records we achieved are 11, 73 and 234 seconds in the following 3 degrees of difficulty: "beginner", "intermediate" and "expert".

One hit every
second

System Administration

The main tasks of the classic Unix system administrator are to maintain and update computers and networks that may have hundreds of users. Though you probably don't have such a great responsibility with your own computer, you cannot completely do without system administration.

Networks with many users

It may be that you want to install new software packages, reconfigure the system kernel, update to a new version or prepare your computer for connection to a network. In any case you need to know what steps are necessary and which parts of the system will be affected.

Keeping the system up to date

LISA can help you for many standard tasks, but there are also a number of cases in which you have to make adjustments by hand. In many cases it will do no harm to know which steps are necessary.

Standard tasks and special cases

In this chapter we want to explain the most important routine tasks and give you enough background knowledge so that you are able to successfully master the necessary system administration.

Routine jobs

6.1 The Right Editor

The topic of text editor should not be pushed aside when talking about system administration. Of course, you can draw upon LISA in many situations and save yourself the use of an editor. But as you may know, there are still some tasks for which it is practical to use an editor.

What was the editor for, again?

There are a great number of editors, which can be used within the command shell.

- **ed** and **red** (restricted ed) are classic line orientated editors, which are not very convenient for the unexperienced user.

- **jed**, a comprehensive, colorful editor with a special C mode, masters not only an Emacs but also a Wordstar emulation, and is also available for OS/2 and DOS.

- **joe**. **jstar**, **jmacs**, **rjoe** and **jpico** are links[1] to **joe**, which start the editor with different characterists. **joe** is a "modeless" editor, which implies that it will not cause beginners too many problems.

- **easyedit**, an editor which, as its name indicates, is easy to use. However, it requires Emacs.

- **elvis** provides the functionality of **vi** and **ex**.

- **vim** (vi improved) is an extended **vi**, which is in the process of gaining acceptance.

- **nvi** (new vi) is a **vi** variant on BSD.

- **vi**, **view**, and **ex** are usually links to one of the previous three editors.

Links for different behaviour

As we already hinted in the list above, some editors are just links, which are used to run an editor in different modes. For example **view** starts **vi** editor in read-only mode i.e for viewing texts. **jstar** starts the editor **joe** in a mode compatible to Wordstar.[2]

Vim for working efficiently

Which editor you want to use in the end is of course just a matter of preference. For day to day editing we prefer **vim** (vi improved, Fig. 6.1). **vim** is an extension of the classic **vi** editor. If you have never before worked with **vi** though, you will at first be quite frustated until you master the basic commands. When working with **vi** you really have to differentiate between two absolutely different modes, the command mode and the insert mode.

Vi command and insert modes

vi starts in the command mode. That means you can enter commands, but no text. The **i** command (insert), amongst others, switches **vi** to insert mode. The **ESC** key sets the editor back to command mode. If you want to save the current text and close the editor use **:x** (exit). To quit without saving the changes use **:q** (quit).

Insert mode

To begin with you should use the tutorial for **vim** (under **/usr/ doc/vim**) and the integrated online help. The advantage of **vim** lies in its powerful commands, which make it possible to work very efficiently. With the help of regular expressions you can, for example, carry out very complicated search and replace processes, edit several files simultaneously, and move very quickly and efficiently within comprehensive texts.

Vim Tutorial

Regular expressions

---

[1] A link points to another file. There are softlinks, which just point to a file, and hardlinks, which are steady 1:1 links to a file.
[2] A program can find out the name used to run it, thereby allowing it to select its characteristic behaviour.

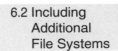

```
─┌──────────────────────────────────────────────────────────┐·─┐
 │                           xterm                          │·│□│
 ├──────────────────────────────────────────────────────────┴─┤
▓│                  VIM help file index                VIM 3.0│
▓│                                                            │
 │RETURN quit help           VIM stands for Vi IMproved.      │
 │ SPACE  one page forward   Most of VIM was made by Bram Moolenaar.│
 │     a  go to this index                                    │
 │     b  one page backward                                   │
 │                                                            │
 │c  left-right and up-down motions   q  options i-n          │
 │d  word and text object motions     r  options p-s          │
 │e  pattern searches                 s  options s-t          │
 │f  various motions; using tags      t  options t-y          │
 │g  scrolling                        u  undo; shell; quickfix; various│
 │h  inserting text; digraphs         v  command line editing │
 │i  insert mode                      w  Ex ranges; Ex special characters│
 │j  changing text                    x  editing files        │
 │k  complex changes                  y  using the file list  │
 │l  deleting, copying, moving text   z  writing and quitting │
 │m  repeating commands               A  starting VIM         │
 │n  key mapping; abbreviations       B  multi window functions│
 │o  option commands, options a-c     C  buffer list functions│
 │p  options d-h                                              │
 │                                                            │
 │Read "reference.doc" for a more complete explanation.       │
▓│            <space = next; return = quit; a = index; b = back>█│
 └──────────────────────────────────────────────────────────────┘
```

Fig. 6.1: The **vim** text editor.

The use of **joe** or **easyedit** is much easier as they function rather like of the editors from DOS or Windows. It will be best to try each editor and to decide on the one which appeals most to you, with respect to its use.

Simple editing with easyedit

Besides the editors for the text consoles or the **xterm** there are also pure X11 editors, of course.

X11 editors

- **xedit**, a simple and clear X11 editor, whose advanced functions can be controlled via keyboard commands.

- **xjed**, the X11 version of the **jed** editor.

- **asWedit**, meant as editor for HTML 2 and HTML 3 documents, which can also be used as a normal text editor of course.

- **xemacs**, the king of the editors.

Of these, **xedit**, due to its clarity, is the best for beginners and **xemacs** is the best and only choice for professionals.

For the beginning: xedit

6.2 Including Additional File Systems

Aside of the root file system, which is integrated (mounted) automatically under **/** each time the system starts, there may be a number of additional file systems, that you want to access either continually or from time to time. These can be further Linux, DOS or OS/2 partitions, and also CD-ROM drives and diskettes.

Access to addtional file systems

File system support

For Linux partitions, the file system support has to be contained directly in the kernel.[3] For other file systems it may be necessary to activate the corresponding support by loading the matching kernel module.

Linux offers support for almost every common PC file system. The following are some of the file systems that can be given as a type when mounting:

- **ext2** for a Linux extended 2 file system,

- **ext** for an old Linux extended file system,

- **nfs** for a network file system (NFS),

- **minix** for a Minix file system (e.g. common for Linux boot diskettes),

- **iso9660 or isofs**[4] for a ISO9660 CD-ROM file system,

- **hpfs** for a OS/2 high performance file system (HPFS), and

- **msdos** for a DOS or OS/2 FAT file system.

Integrating by hand or automatically

Besides the most obvious possibility of integrating file systems by hand with the corresponding **mount** command, it is also possible to integrate certain file systems in your root file system during the boot process or automatically on demand.

So, there are three very different ways of integrating file systems:

- manually with the **mount** command,

- automatically with the help of the mount table **/etc/fstab** and

- automatically via the automount daemon **amd**.

Mountung only possible as superuser

As only the superuser can call up the **mount** command, we will first show you how to automatically integrate further file systems with the help of the mount table or the **amd** so that also a normal user also may have access to it.

---

[3] Otherwise the root file system could not be mounted after the boot process and the system could not start at all. By the way, the same problem occurs when it is not possible to load the support for the SCSI controller, which controls the hard disk with your root partition.

[4] It is valid for almost every other kernel module for file system support, that the name of the module corresponds to the file system type for the **mount** command. In this case though, the name of the module differs with **isofs**.

6.2.1 The Mount Table /etc/fstab

Each file system to be mounted automatically while booting is entered
in the file **/etc/fstab**.

You can specify, via options, whether the listed file systems will be *Mount options*
mounted immediately upon system start, or only prepared for mounting.
Although, in the second case, the respective file system is not intergrated *Simplifying the*
while booting, since the system already knows details about it, mount- *mounting*
ing can be carried out by giving just one detail, such as the mount point
or device name, to the **mount** command.

The necessary entries to **/etc/fstab** can either be made by hand *Making entries*
or be configured with the help of LISA in the menu "system configura- *with LISA*
tion" with the item "mount table".

In order to be able to integrate a file system within the root file *Necessary options*
system the following details are required:

- the type of file system type to be mounted (fstype), e.g. **minix**,
  ext2 or **msdos**,

- options, like for example **ro** (readonly) or **rw** (readwrite),

- the location (special device name) of the file system to be mounted, as for example a partition or an NFS directory, and

- the location at which the file system is to be integrated (node),
  e.g. **/mnt** or **/mnt/cdrom**.

A mount command is usually called up then in the form

```
mount -t fstype -o option device node
```

This call can then, as we have already hinted, be automated or
prepared via the mount table.

We will briefly explain the construction of this mount table *Structure of an*
(Fig. 6.2). An entry of the file **/etc/fstab** is put together ac- *fstab entry*
cording to the following scheme:

device   mount point   type   options   dump flag   checkfs flag

The corresponding device file is set as device and the directory under
which the file system is to be integrated is set as the mount point. There
are a number of possible options. The most common are:

- **defaults** – corresponds to the options **rw**, **suid**, **dev**, **exec**,
  auto, **nouser** and **async**,

- **ro** – readonly (reading access only),

- **rw** – readwrite (reading and writing access),

- **user** – the file system can also be mounted by normal users,

- **noauto** – the entered file system is not mounted automatically, when starting the system (e.g. for diskettes or CD-ROM),

- **noexec** – no binary programs can be carried out by this file system (important for foreign architectures),

- **sync** – each I/O operation is carried out synchronously only (safer), and

- **nosuid** – Set User ID or Set Group ID has no effect.

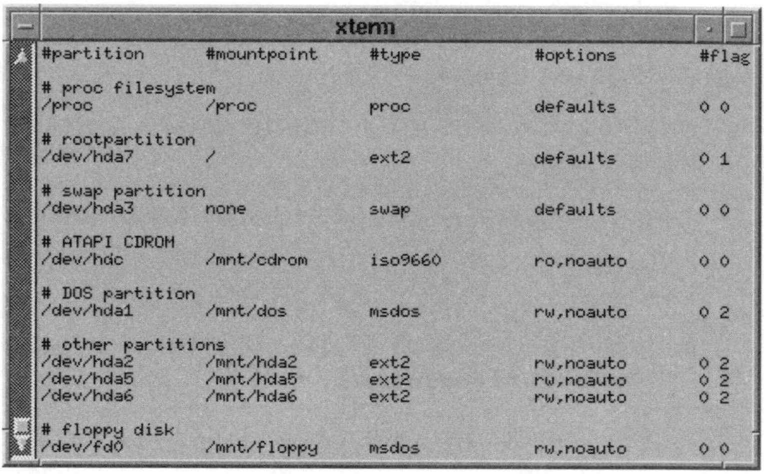

```
┌─────────────────────────────────────────────────────────────┐
│ ─                          xterm                        ·  □ │
├─────────────────────────────────────────────────────────────┤
│▲│#partition       #mountpoint    #type        #options    #flag
│ │
│ │# proc filesystem
│ │/proc            /proc          proc         defaults     0 0
│ │
│ │# rootpartition
│ │/dev/hda7        /              ext2         defaults     0 1
│ │
│ │# swap partition
│ │/dev/hda3        none           swap         defaults     0 0
│ │
│ │# ATAPI CDROM
│ │/dev/hdc         /mnt/cdrom     iso9660      ro,noauto    0 0
│ │
│ │# DOS partition
│ │/dev/hda1        /mnt/dos       msdos        rw,noauto    0 2
│ │
│ │# other partitions
│ │/dev/hda2        /mnt/hda2      ext2         rw,noauto    0 2
│ │/dev/hda5        /mnt/hda5      ext2         rw,noauto    0 2
│ │/dev/hda6        /mnt/hda6      ext2         rw,noauto    0 2
│▼│# floppy disk
│ │/dev/fd0         /mnt/floppy    msdos        rw,noauto    0 0
└─────────────────────────────────────────────────────────────┘
```

Fig. 6.2: The structure of the mount table **/etc/fstab**.

Dump flag

The dump flag indicates whether or not the respective file system is to be saved by the backup program **dump**. If this field is missing, a 0 is assumed. A 1 tells **dump** to save the file system.

Checkfs Flag

The checkfs flag is utilized by the file system checking program, which is activated automatically every time the system is started. The root file system has to be given the number 1, and all further file systems which are to be checked are given a 2 or greater. A 0 is entered for file systems which need not or should not be checked. If you change the

Changes are only valid after rebooting

entries, your changes are only activated after rebooting.

Now we'll give you some examples of how the entries for **/etc/ fstab** should look:

- for **/dev/hda3** as a Linux ext2 file system mounted at **/home**:

/dev/hda3 /home ext2 defaults 1 2

- for **/dev/hdb1** as a DOS partition mounted at **/dos**:

  `/dev/hdb1 /dos msdos defaults 0 2`

- for **/export** from the computer **1st** mounted at **/import**:

  `1st:/export /import nfs defaults 0 0`

- for a CD in the Mitsumi CD ROM drive (**/dev/mcd**) mounted to **/cdrom**:

  `/dev/mcd /cdrom iso9660 ro 0 0`

- for a CD in the SCSI CD ROM drive (**/dev/sr0**) mounted to **/cdrom**:

  `/dev/sr0 /cdrom iso9660 ro,noauto 0 0`

- for **/dev/hdb2** as swap partition:

  `/dev/hdb2 none swap 0 0`

The **proc** file system is an exception and must always be entered in **/etc/fstab**. So, never change this entry. The **proc** file system is mounted under the directory **/proc**, where you can find information on the system and on all existing processes.

The Proc file system

6.2.2 The Automount Daemon amd

The daemon **amd** (automount daemon) provides a further, convenient way of automatically integrating additional file systems. It offers two special advantages.

Automatic mounting on demand

- You don't need, as usual, any superuser rights for the mount process. This means that a normal user can mount a file system.

- The mounting of the respective file systems is carried out automatically, whenever necessary. This will always be the case, when the working directory is changed to one that is not mounted, but which is known to the **amd**. The **amd** also unmounts any file system it has mounted, as soon as all users have left that file system.

At the moment, when using the default setting, the CD-ROM drive and DOS or Linux formatted diskettes are integrated under the path **/auto** by the **amd** the first time a user changes the subdirectory

The /auto directory

117

(**/auto/cdrom** or **/auto/floppy**) respectively. If there is no user working in the directory any more, then it is automatically unmounted by **amd** again.

Electronic
diskette
eject

Unfortunately there are still no PCs which offer diskette drives with electronic eject, as is the case for SUN workstations or Apple Macintosh. Therefore there is always the risk that a user takes a mounted diskette from the diskette drive before it has been unmounted. This means the diskette's file system can be in an inconsistent state when the diskette is removed.

Contolled
diskette
removal

Even the operating system will only notice that the diskette is no longer in the drive, when a write or read access is fails. With an electronic diskette drive, the removal of the diskette can be prevented by the operating system until the file system in question has been unmounted. You may notice that some CD-ROM drives have electronic control.

6.2.3 Mounting a Filesystem with the mount Command

Mounting
manually

If you want to integrate a certain file system temporarily then, as superuser, you can just carry it out manually with the **mount** command. The corresponding **mount** commands for the examples shown in the section on mount tables are listed below. Notice that the list does not include an equivalent for the proc file system and that the swap partion is mounted with **swapon**.

```
mount -t ext2 /dev/hda3 /home
mount -t msdos /dev/hdb1 /dos
mount -t nfs 1st:/export /import
mount -t iso9660 -o ro /dev/mcd /cdrom
mount -t iso9660 -o ro /dev/sr0 /cdrom
swapon /dev/hdb2
```

6.3 User Administration

Multi-user
operating system

Linux is a multi-user operating system, which means several users can be known to the system. These users can simultaneously log into and work with the system. There are several elements for each user of the system:

- an entry in the password file **/etc/passwd**,

- an entry in the shadow password file **/etc/shadow**, if the shadow password system is used,

- membership of a user group, which has to be entered in the user group file **/etc/group** and

- a home directory, which bears the name of the user, and in which the user is entitled to write.

If LISA didn't make these entries, you would have to have knowledge of the structure of the password file. An entry in the password file is made up of following components:

Construction of the password file

- the login name, that is the name under which the user is known to the system;

- optionally the encoded password. When the shadow password system is used there is a "*****" in place of the password and the real password is held in the file **/etc/shadow**;

- the user ID, a whole number, which is unique;

- the group ID, the number of the user group, to which the user belongs;

- name of the user and other real world information on the person, like first name and surname, telephone number, and room number;

- the home directory, the absolute path to the user's home directory;

- the shell, that is the command interpreter, which is started when the user logs in.

The the individual fields are separated by colons. An example entry could look as follows:

Fields separated by colons

```
sarah:*:1234:100:Sarah Becker,,,:/home/sarah:/bin/bash
```

If there is further information on the user, aside the name, like the room number or telephone number, these are contained between the commas after the real name of the user.

Further information on the user

The entry for the shell of the user is recorded in the variable $SHELL and the entry for the home directory in the variable $HOME. By the way, the entry in the password file doesn't have to be a shell program. It can also be any program to be run when the user logs in.

User shell

So, you could create a user named **shutdown**, whose "shell" entry is merely a script which checks that no other users are logged in, then shutdown the computer.

A user named shutdown

Now let's take a look at the password file entry for the superuser in a system without shadow passwords:

`root:tL4a6r80yzhXE:0:0:Super User:/root:/bin/bash`

You can see there, that he or she has the user ID 0 as well as the group ID 0. Both are reserved for the superuser and provide him or her with maximum rights in the system. The encoded password is displayed and readable. In the next section you will learn that this is a security hole.

User and group ID 0

6.4   The Shadow Password System

The shadow password system, in comparison to the common password system, offers additional security as the file **/etc/shadow** contains the encoded passwords, but in contrary to the file **/etc/passwd**, is not readable by everybody. It stands, so to speak, "in the shadows".

Additional security

The coding function **crypt**, used to encode passwords, is a one-way function. It can only be used in one direction. This means the password entered at the password prompt is encoded by **crypt** and the result is compared with the entry in the password file.

One-way function

In other words, there is no function able to uncode passwords from the password file, without requiring a lot of effort.

There are special programs, like for example **crack** which, with the help of dictionaries and by combinations, encode possible passwords with **crypt**. Then they compare the result with the encoded passwords from the password file, until they find corresponding ones, which means they can crack certain passwords. **SATAN** is of course a tool to be used by system administrators for the purpose of checking the security of their systems.

Cracking passwords with crack

If you don't use a shadow password system, the encoded passwords can be gathered by or passed on by any user. Even if encoded passwords are difficult to crack, the security hole exists, because if he has the encoded passwords, a hacker has all the time he wants to crack them. Poorly chosen passwords only make the problem worse.[5]

Security hole

---

[5] For a while there was a snowball system operating via Internet email which asked people to send their passwords to a particular address. There were surely inexperienced people who did just this. We clarified the intention of the snowball sender earier.

6.5 NIS Network Information Service

The network information service (NIS), still often known as "yp" (yellow pages)[6], provides an elegant method of making information relevant to a number of computer available network wide. This can be password or host files as well as particular computer resources.

Yellow Pages

In principle, NIS is realised by a simple, distributed database, which mainly serves the purpose of simplifying the system and network administration.

NIS database

In larger networks of Unix computers, changing the system files for user administration and information on network wide resources, then distributing them manually to all computers of the network is usually a very monotonous task prone to errors.

Network resources

In addition, partly inaccessible computers, completely switched off computers, and different operating system installations make it all the more difficult to regularly manually update these data from a central computer.

If you think this matter over, you will see that the expenditure of energy and time will rise quadratically to the number of users and computers, as normally each user and each computer should be known by all other computers.

Quadratic expenditure of energy and time without NIS

NIS provides a simple mechanism for coping with the administration of user and hardware resources in Unix networks with linearly increasing effort, that means in proportion to the number of users or to the number of the linked computers.

Less expenditure of time for the administration

6.5.1 NIS Domain Names

In order to be able to delimit separately administered subnets within a larger network, every NIS action is carried out within a domain. The name of this domain only has to be unique in the local vicinity in order to maintain clarity at the interfaces between the subnets, such as routers or common file servers.

NIS domains

This domain name is not to be confused with the hierarchical DNS names (see7.2.6), which have to be unique across the whole internet. In contrast to globally unique area names, for example "lisa.lst.de", a simple NIS domain name like "net1", "localnet" or "lst-work" would be sufficient for the delimitation from other subnets or networks.

Do not mix up the NIS domains with DNS

With the **domainname** command, the name of the NIS domain can be set by the superuser and be obtained by every normal user.

Domainname

---

[6] The original name "yellow pages (YP)" actually had to be changed when British Telecom sued. However the name still appears in program code and documentation.

6.5.2   Information Exchange

Administration of
whole network
hierarchies
Server side

To show the basic features of NIS, we will limit our explanations to just one network with a single server. In principle though, it is possible to administer a whole hierarchy of servers and subservers with NIS.

It would be best to approach NIS from both sides, the server side and the client side. The server administers the information and provides it to the client computers.

The NIS server in the main includes three components:

- the configuration files, which are available to the network and are located under **/etc**, like for example **/etc/hosts** or **/etc/passwd**,

- the corresponding databases, which are under **/var/nis/<domainname>/*** and

- the program **ypserv**, which provides this database to the network.

Generating
with make

Usually one creates the database files with the **make** program, both after the setting of NIS, and after each change to the source files. The database tables consist of simple key/value string pairs. So, when there are source files with several search keys, like the **passwd** file, an new file is created for each search key. In this case these are **passwd.byname** for looking up a user name and for finding the corresponding user ID and **passwd.byuid** for the reverse direction. These file names, by the way, are a convention, and are compiled into many client programs.

Passwd.byname
and passwd.byuid

RPC calls

The **ypserv** program works on network inquiries in the form of Remote Procedure Calls (RPCs). A request consists of the domain name, the file name and the searched key. A positive answer contains the corresponding "value" of the file.

On the client side there are two main components:

- the **ypbind** program, controlling the link connection to the server and

- the C runtime library (**libc**), whose routines read the **/etc/*** files and in some circumstances also make RPCs to the NIS server.

Continual
connection

For performance reasons, **ypbind** continually maintains the connection to the next NIS server and provides local programs with its address before a NIS inquiry. This is necessary as NIS can be configured for redundancy, i.e, there can be secondary NIS servers and hence the server address may change during operation if the primary server is unreachable.

To get further information on NIS, we recommend to you the manual pages of the associated programs as well as the Linux NIS-HOWTO (it is to be found under **/usr/doc/HOWTO**).

6.6 The Printing Subsystem

Unix systems normally use the **lpr** printing subsystem for controlling and managing printers. **lpr** makes it possible:

- to control access to several printers,

- to spool printing requests,

- to administer the printing request queue,

- to gain network wide access to printer resources, and

- to use printing filters, for preparing various file formats for printing.

For this purpose, a number of special commands are available, for example:

- **lpr**, to send printing requests to the printing subsystem,

- **lpq**, for listing all print requests in the queue,

- **lprm**, to remove printing requests from the queue,

- **lpc**, to administer the printing resources, specified in **/etc/printcap**, and

- **lpd**, the printing subsystem daemon responsible for controlling and carrying out the printing requests.

All details on printer resources, that is which printers are connected, which names they respond to, and which formats they can print, are set in the file **/etc/printcap**. The entries in this file can vary greatly, so we suggest you read the **printcap** manual page and Printing-HOWTO.

For the configuration of the printing subsystem POWER LINUX uses the new LPR-ng package, which initializes the printing subsystem, installs a number of very useful filters and enters them in **/etc/printcap**. LPR-ng is automatically activated with the default settings, during installation of POWER LINUX.

These filters are very important when you want to print PostScript files on a printer, which doesn't directly support PostScript. Under

Linux this is possible without any problem with the appropriate filter and **ghostscript** (see 5.3.1).

As an example, to save paper, you can reduce and print several pages onto a single physical printing page, when using a filter.

Printer daemon lpd

The printer daemon **lpd** has a special status within the list of the printer programs. It is activated automatically, when the system starts and remains in the background, ready to receive and carry out printing orders from **lpr**.

Usually you will not need to call up this daemon by hand. When you have problems though, you should check whether or not **lpd** is active:

```
root@lisa:~# ps aux | grep lpd | grep -v grep
root     66 0.0 0.2 872 36 ? S 08:02 0:00 (lpd)
root@lisa:~#
```

*Starting **lpd**
by hand*

If this wasn't the case, you can try to start it again by hand with the command **/usr/sbin/lpd**. Normally there will still be other reasons why **lpd** doesn't run. You could also find a clue in the directory **/var/spool/lpd**.

Network printer

If you want to use a printer via the network, that means from several computers, you must give these computers access to the printing subsystem with the file **/etc/hosts.lpd**, and you must enter this printer as remote printer in the **printcap** file.

The printers of your system are also directly accessible as device files **/dev/lp***, that means with the command,

```
cat filename > /dev/lp1
```

you can send files directly to the printer, thus avoiding the printing subsystem.

*Staircase effect
with HP printers*

When you have HP compatible printers and printing results in the "staircase" effect, you have either to change the printer settings for line feed or better use the default printer **lp** of the **lpr** printing subsystem.

In principle though, you should always print via the **lpr** printing subsystem, if possible. To use PostScript efficiently, or if several users are using the printer simultaneously, you will no longer do without this printing subsystem.

6.7   Administration of Software Components

*Structuring by
single software
packages*

The software components, of which your Linux system is composed, are structured in single software packages, which mostly contain a certain application or program groups. This division has the advantage that you can selectively install particular programs or remove them from the system.

The "tar archive" is probably still the most common package format. The name tar archive is due to the fact that these archives are created with the **tar** command.[7] We will describe the possibilities of the GNU **tar** command next.

Tar archive

The advantage of the tar archive lies in its simple use. The disadvantage is that it is very difficult to add ancilliary information to its contents. Because of this, further package formats have established themselves recently. These packages can contain much more information about the contents, the use of packages or the dependencies amongst the packages.

Simple use of tar

The most flexible concept at present, is offered by the Red Hat package format, named "rpm". Together with the **rpm** program it offers comprehensive possibilities for administrating and maintaining software components in the system.

rpm format

LST Linux has long been founded on the traditional tar archives, but after considering the benefits with respect to future growth and development, we decided to convert it to the rpm format.

Better opportunity for development

6.7.1 Compressed Tar Archives

As the greater part of the Linux and Unix software is still offered in the tar format on the various FTP sites, we will first examine them in more depth, before moving on to describe the new rpm format in the next section.

Tar is still very common

Tar archives are most often made available in a compressed form. Compressing has the advantage that the data then occupies only the absolute minimum space. Furthermore, less data have to be transferred across networks, and when compressed with the **gzip** program, a check sum is created for the package. With this check sum, the integrity of the package can easily be tested.

Compressed tar archive

An uncompressed tar archive usually has the suffix **.tar**. Compressing the archive with the **gzip** program, will by default append the suffix **.gz**, and so results in the ending **.tar.gz**. For compatibility with the 8+3 DOS file names this ending is often abbreviated to **.tgz**.

tgz ending

Some old packages will still have the ending **.z**. Such packages are not compressed with the modern **gzip** program, but with the older Unix program **compress**. This will not cause irritation, as **gzip** unpacks the older **compress** format, without further assistance.

.Z ending

For better understanding we'll give you an example. Let's suppose, you have copied the package **xmelt.tgz** from the directory

Sunsite FTP server

---

[7] Under Linux usually the GNU **tar** program is used. It has greater functionality than the original Unix **tar**. The command name **tar** comes from "Tape ARchive".

Checking
the archive

pub/Linux/X11/toys of the sunsite FTP server (ftp://sunsite.unc.
edu). A mirror, that is a copy, of the directory sunsite.unc.edu/pub/Linux
is included in the second POWER LINUX CD-ROM.

You can now first of all check, whether the archive has been
correctly transferred. For this purpose you enter the command:

```
gzip -tv xmelt.tgz
```

If the archive is OK, you are given the message

```
xmelt.tgz:      OK
```

Work mode

The **tar** command is controlled by a great number of options. Take
the time to have a look at the manual page to **tar**. The **tar** command
has to be run each time with one of the working mode options. The most
significant are:

c	(create):	creates a new archive
x	(extract):	unpacks an existing archive
t	(table of contents):	lists the contents of an archive
r	(append):	appends files
		to the end of an archive
d	(diff):	finds differences between achive
		and file system

Options

Furthermore there are a number of important options which can be
combined with the working mode:

f	(filename):	file name of the archive
z	(compress):	works on compressed archives
v	(verbose):	gives verbose messages
M	(multivolume):	works on archives spread over several
		media (e.g. diskettes)
T	(files from):	states a file, in which the files
		to be archived are listed.

Considerable
number of options

From **tar --help** or the manual page to **tar** you can obtain a
complete overview of **tar**'s options. Don't be deterred by the number
of options – **tar** is a very powerful tool.

To see what's in the archive **xmelt.tgz** enter the command:

```
tar tzvf xmelt.tgz
```

A list of the files contained in the archive will be displayed. The
above command produced the following output:

```
drwx------ root/root    00000 xmelt/
-rw------- root/root    00175 xmelt/README.linux
-rwx------ root/root    13316 xmelt/xmelt
```

If you now want to unpack the files in your current working directory, this will be done with the **tar** option **x**. With the command:

tar xzvf xmelt.tgz

*Unpacking
the archive*

the directory **xmelt** is created, and the files **README.linux** and **xmelt** are placed in it. When unpacking tar archives make sure, that their contents don't overwrite existing files in your file system by mistake. So, first of all list the contents of an archive, and check where you are in the file system, before unpacking an archive. Sometimes it is also recommended that you unpack archives in a specially created subdirectory. From there you can selectively re-copy or re-locate the files as needed.

*Enumerating
the contents*

If you want to create a tar archive yourself, you need to use the **c** option. After the file name of the archive to be created comes a list of files or directories to be included in the archive.

*Creating
an archive*

Creating new archives makes sense especially when you want to save configuration files that you have altered. Let's suppose you want to save the files:

/usr/X11R6/lib/X11/Xconfig
/usr/X11R6/lib/X11/xinit/xinitrc
/home/user/guest/.Xdefaults

in an archive called **config.tgz**. First it is recommended that you make a list of these files in a special file (e.g. **filelist**). You can either do this with an editor or divert the output from the **find** command into a file, which can be much more efficient and gives you exactly the filenames desired. Once **filelist** contains the list of all files you wanted included in the archive, the command

*Preparing
the file list*

tar czvfT config.tgz filelist

creates the desired archive **config.tgz**. Be sure that you run your version of the above command at the appropriate place in the file system, that is the position that fits with the paths stated in your **filelist**.

It is easier to save a complete directory (including all subdirectories) in an archive. This is done with the command

*Saving the
directory*

tar czvf archiv.tgz directory

As a handy check, the **v** option causes the names of files to be listed as they are added to the archive.

Of course, device files (special devices) can be used as the target file as, under Unix, these are no different to "normal" files. So, with the command

```
tar czvf /dev/fd0 directory
```

Saving the archive on diskette

the tar archive is written onto diskette from the start. To read it in again, you again have to state the device filename instead of a normal filename:

```
tar xzvf /dev/fd0
```

Multivolume archive

If you want to create an archive larger than a single diskette, then use the **M** (Multi-volume) option. Note, however, that compression (i.e. the **z** option) cannot be used.

```
tar cMvf /dev/fd0 directory
```

When the first diskette is full, **tar** requires further diskettes (volume) until the archive is completely written.

Combination with find

If you combine this **tar** command with the **find** command, you can easily save a selection of files on diskette. If, for example, at the end of the installation, the file **/install/END** was the last to be created and contains a list of all other files on the system, the command

```
find / -newer /install/END -type f | tar cMvfT /dev/fd0 -
```

saves all files of the complete file system on diskette, which have been changed after installation.

Input via the pipe

In this example notice the "**-**" sign which indicates that the data is to be read from the pipe **|**, that is, from the output of the **find** command.

Simple complete backup

As you could easily re-establish the state of things up to the end of the installation by installing again, you have in this way created a quick "complete backup" of your system. Life can be so easy under Linux!

6.7.2   Red Hat Package Management

New de facto standard

The Red Hat **rpm** package format has succeded in becomming a new de facto standard within a short time. The reason for this lies in the open development of **rpm** and in the great possibilities that use of the **rpm** presents.

Independent development

Even though the "r" in **rpm** stands for Red Hat, it is a completely open software packaging system independent from Red Hat. It has its own developer channel and can be freely used by everyone.

Comprehensive mechanisms

Aside from providing features comparable to those of **tar**, **rpm** also includes mechanisms for updating software packages, system wide packages registration, consistence checking, and administration of software components. As well, **rpm** handles source code and whole program groups or subpackages uniformly.

The great number of features offered by **rpm** shows itself in the user interface. Provided that one is accustomed to the use of the **tar** command, one can relatively easily and without ancilliary features, access the content of tar archives. At first sight the same tasks appear to be more difficult with the **rpm**. But even working with **rpm** packages is not so difficult, once you know how to operate the **rpm**.

One has to get accustomed to the operation

Maybe there is some confusion regarding the use of the expression "rpm". "rpm" is the name for the package format as well as for the **rpm** program, with which one administers **rpm** packages. It is analogous to the situtation with tar archives, which are administered with the **tar** program, with the exception that tar archives are often also compressed and have the suffix **.tgz** or **.tar.gz**.

Rpm names the program as well as the packages

rpm packages are also compressed, by the way. Since the package is always compressed there is no need to indicate this in the suffix.

You have several methods of administering software components of your system at your disposal. You can use the "software administration" area of LISA, operate **rpm** directly from the command line, or use Red Hat's graphical installation tool **glint** frontend for the **rpm**.

Different possibilities for software administration

In Fig. 6.3 you can see the division into several program groups under **glint**. This division under **glint** is well structured and is simple in its use. But if you want to work on the information that can be provided by **rpm** you should get used to the operation of **rpm**.

Glint

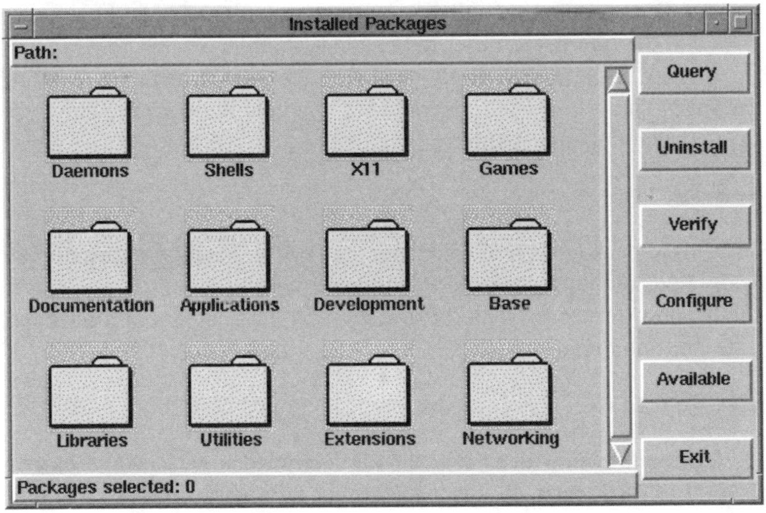

Fig. 6.3: The **glint** tool for package administration.

Let's get a general idea on the use of **rpm**. **rpm**'s command line options can be divided into five main categories:

Main areas

- The install mode: **-i** or **--install**
- The erase mode: **-e** or **--erase**
- The query mode: **-q** or **--query**
- The update mode: **-U** or **--update**
- The verify mode: **-V** or **--verify**

Install mode

Let's begin with the install mode. If you want to install for example the **lisa-2.0.1.i386.rpm** package on your system, this is done with the command

```
rpm -i lisa-2.0-1.i386.rpm
```

Rpm database

Thereby the contents of the package are installed and this action is recorded in the **rpm** database. The **rpm** also checks the database to see whether the package has been installed already. If this is the case, you just get a message saying that the package already exists in the system.

Installation via ftp

An extremely interesting feature of **rpm** is the possibility to directly install packages via ftp, if you are linked to the Internet. So, one saves the effort of transfering and locally storing a package. With the command

```
rpm -i ftp://ftp.1st.de/pub/install/lisa-2.0-1.i386.rpm
```

this is all done automatically. As already mentioned, you have to be linked to the Internet in order to be able to do this.

Removing packages again

Just as easy as installing new packages, is removal of existing packages from the system. Should for example the package above be deleted again, then just enter

```
rpm -e lisa
```

and the package is removed from the system. Thereby **rpm** automatically finds out the right version number by itself.

Contents of a package

If you want to get some information on the contents of a package, enter the command

```
rpm -ql lisa
```

Overview on all packages

It provides you with a list of the files included in the package **lisa-2.0-1.i386.rpm**. If you want to get an overview of all installed packages, use the options **-qia**, which give you a list of all (**-a**) information (**-i**) on the installed packages.

List of all files

If you use the option **-l** instead of **-i**, i.e. you run **rpm -qla**, you get a list of all files existing in the system. You have to expect that the output of this call will be very long.

But there is the practical Unix command **grep**, through which one can easily filter things in order to keep the output comprehensible. For example, if you are interested in the list of all PostScript documents installed in the system, you should try the following command:

Overview with grep

```
rpm -qla | grep 'ps' | less
```

You could argue, that you can get the list with the **find / -name** *'*.ps*'* command too. The asterisk after **ps** provides you not only with the files, which end with **.ps**, but also the ones which are compressed, i.e. those whose names end with **.ps.gz** or **.psz**. **find** will need much more time though, and when additional NFS file systems are mounted such a simple **find** command cannot be recommended at all.

Find isn't always an alternative

For this purpose the **rpm** database offers clear advantages, as it is always kept up to date. Of course this is only possible, as long as you haven't installed or removed files by hand. Naturally the **rpm** database couldn't know anything about these actions.

Updated database

A further feature of **rpm** is the upgrade mechanism. With the command

```
rpm -U lisa-2.1-1.i386.rpm
```

an existing package can be upgraded by a new version, without causing problems. The old version is removed correctly by **rpm**.

rpm also offers the interesting possibility of verifying the system. Thereby the location, the type, and the size of files are checked against the **rpm** database. Even the contents of the file can be checked by using the checksums.

Verification of the system

You can use this to check a particular file, a certain package or even the whole system. The **rpm** database serves as reference as to how the individual components should be arranged in your system. So you can find all files in the system, which differ from the details recorded in the database, with the command

Checking certain files

```
rpm -Va
```

To run this check for a single package, in place of **-a**, use **-p** followed by the package name, and for a single file use **-f** followed by a filename.

Besides the **rpm** command, POWER LINUX also contains three special tools which are extremly practical when one doesn't want to install a package into the system, but rather needs information on the package.

Special POWER
LINUX *tools*

- **rpmextr** extracts information from the package,

- **rpmshow** lists the files included in the package, and

- **rpminst** unpacks the files included in the package to the current directory.

You will always obtain a use message for the commands, if you run them with the option **--help**.

6.8   The Use of fdisk for Experts

BIOS limitations

Using large hard disks in the PC may expose certain problems caused by the historic limitations of the IDE standard and BIOS.

CHS model

On the one hand, the traditional PC BIOS can only handle hard disks with a maximum of 256 heads, 63 sectors and 1024 cylinders, and on the other hand the IDE standard allows a maximum of 16 heads, 255 sectors and up to 65536 cylinders according to the CHS (Cylinders, Heads, Sectors) model. The intersection of both results in 16 heads, 63 sectors and 1024 cylinders and a maximium size of just 504MB.

LBA - logical block addressing

The newer Enhanced IDE standard avoids this limitation, by simply consecutively numbering all sectors on the disk with the logical block addressing (LBA) technique.

Extended CHS model

The second method of avoiding this limitation is offered by the extended XCHS model supported by newer BIOS versions. This model extends the number of possible heads to 256. Both possibilities result in a limit of almost 7.9 GB.

Boot parameter for EIDE

(E)IDE should not actually cause any problems when using Linux with large disks. If difficulties do arise though, try first to pass on the actual values for your hard disk to the (E)IDE driver with the boot parameter **hdx=cyl,heads,sect** (where **hdx** stands for **hda** up to **hdd**). By doing so you can prevent Linux obtaining the wrong hard disk parameters from the PC BIOS.

No BIOS limits under Linux

Read through the following paragraphs to learn how to translate the real parameters to obtain less than 1024 cylinders. Linux itself isn't influenced by the limitations of the BIOS, because it has direct access to the hardware, i.e. independent from the BIOS.

LBA mode

SCSI hard disks always use the LBA mode mentioned above. But in contrast to EIDE for hard disks larger than 1GB, there may be the problem that the hard disk parameters have to be adapted for **fdisk** and **lilo**.

Warnings from fdisk

The problem will become evident when **fdisk** gives the corresponding hints and warnings, if you run it during installation (see next paragraph).

/etc/disktab

The translation for **lilo** has to be made with an entry in the file **/etc/disktab**. The translation for **fdisk** has to be made in its

Reading out the partition table when booting

expert mode. We will show you how to apply the theory with an example. The difficulty in the use of large hard disks lies in the fact that the partition table has to be read while booting, i.e. before any operating system is active.

At this stage the boot sector is accessed via the BIOS of the PC, which as mentioned above has the limit of 256 heads, 63 sectors and 1023 cylinders. For this reason the E(IDE) controller attempts to carry out the translation of the hard disk values of hard disks with more than 1023 cylinders in such a way that they are accepted via the BIOS.

Translation of the hard disk values

Fortunately, the partition table itself is always accessible without a problem, as it can be reached via the first cylinder, the first sector, and the first head. This location is independent of any translation scheme and hence it can always be found.

Access to the partition table is always possible

Therefore, while booting there is the limitation that a maximum of 1023 cylinders of the hard disk can be addressed as a result of the BIOS limitation. So, all data needed for the boot process (like for example the bootloader or the operating system kernel) must be located before the 1024th cylinder.

More than 1023 cylinders

Though it is true that you can create partitions without any risk beyond the 1024th cylinder, you cannot boot directly from these partitions. Other operating systems have the same problems.

Booting via 1023 cylinders is not possible

A simple, but not always completely satisfying remedy, is to create the Linux root partition within the 1023 cylinders. It need only contain the kernel and the root file system and can therefore be kept relatively small. 15 MB will be enough.

Linux root partition within 1023 cylinders

The **/usr** partition can then extend beyond the 1024th cylinder. It can be best to create the Linux partitions with the **fdisk** of another operating system (e.g. of OS/2) before you start installing Linux and then while installing Linux, just change the System ID of the desired partitions to the type Linux native (ID 83).

/usr partition beyond 1024th cylinder

A better solution is to give the right combinations of cylinders, sectors and heads in **fdisk** expert mode. The right combinations are those used by the controller and accepted by the BIOS.

Entering correct values in fdisk expert mode

Figure 6.4 shows an example of the translation of the physical parameters of the hard disk to the direct block addressing, which is finally used by the operating system, for communicating with the hard disk.

Hard disk	Hard disk interface	Controller	Operating system
C H S	C H S	C H S	L B A
Physical division in cylinder, heads and sectors	Translation from physical units to logical units (for the controller)	Secondary translation of logical units (for the BIOS)	Translation from logical units to linear block addresses
e.g. 8190/8/128	e.g. 4095/64/32	e.g. 522/255/63	e.g. 0 .. 8385929

Fig. 6.4: BIOS translation of the disk geometry.

Physical division is
not the same as
logical division

SCSI rounded
parameters

LBA

Different
figures

Extended
translation

Translation
of the values

Entering the
right values in
the expert mode

On the left hand side you can see that the physical division of the disk often differs from the logical values displayed. Actually, there are usually much fewer heads on the hard disk than it claims.

The logical values provided by the disk, should remain within the bounds of IDE or BIOS. In the case of an EIDE or SCSI controller, the controller itself will make another translation of the values.

With regard to SCSI, these are most often 64 heads and 32 sectors, as from this division there results a "round" quantity of 64*32*512 bytes = 1 MB for each cylinder. EIDE uses the reserves of the EIDE standard (XCHS model) and increases the number of heads to 255.

The last translation is carried out by the operating system itself. Thereby Linux uses the logical block addressing (LBA), which directly addresses the blocks linearly from the first to the last block on the hard disk.

There are many controllers which use two different schemes for obtaining a value under 1024 for the number of cylinders. First of all the controller usually tries to double the number of heads.

If this doesn't result in a cylinder number less than 1024, the controller increases the values of heads and sectors to the maximum possible number, in order to minimise the number of cylinders.

This procedure corresponds, for example, to the extended translation of the Adaptec controllers AHA 274x/284x/294x. The NCR controllers use a variant in which the number of sectors are chosen just as large as necessary to keep to the limit of 1023 cylinders. Thereby the clipping effected by the creating of partitions will be minimised, as the partitions always start and end exactly at the cylinder boundaries.

The translation of an Adaptec controller, for example, results in a number of 255 heads, 63 sectors, and 522 cylinders. Without this translation **fdisk** states 64 heads, 32 sectors, and 4095 cylinders.

Your task will be to find out what translation is carried out by the controller and to set the values for the hard disk in the expert mode of **fdisk**. Note, that the total capacity of the hard disk must remain constant.

We now want to explain the procedure necessary with an example of an 4 GB SCSI hard disk. This hard disk has more than 1023 cylinders and the Linux **fdisk** gives a warning regarding the disk geometry while installing:

```
The number of cylinders for this disk is set to 4095.
This is larger than 1024, and may cause problems with:

1) software that runs at boot time (e.g., LILO)
2) booting and partitioning software form other OSs
   (e.g., DOS FDISK, OS/2 FDISK)
```

If you want to look at the partition table with **p**, you will see a number of error messages:

```
Device  Boot Begin Start   End   Blocks    Id   System
/dev/sda1   1     1      754   771088+    6   DOS 16-bit>32M
         Partition 1 does not end on cylinder boundary:
         phys=(95, 254, 63) should be (95, 63, 32)
/dev/sda2 *  97    754   1954  1228972+   82   Linux swap
         Partition 2 does not end on cylinder boundary:
         phys=(248, 254, 63) should be (248, 63, 32)
/dev/sda3  1274  1954   2456   514080    a5   BSD/386
         Partition 3 does not end on cylinder boundary:
         phys=(312, 254, 63) should be (312, 63, 32)
/dev/sda4  2362  2456   4095 1678792+    5   Extended
         Partition 4 does not end on cylinder boundary:
         phys=(521, 254, 63) should be (521, 63, 32)
/dev/sda5  2362  2456   2707   257008+   83   Linux
/dev/sda6  2394  2707   2770    64228+   83   Linux native
/dev/sda7  2402  2770   3436   682731     6   DOS 16-bit>32M
/dev/sda8  2487  3436   4095   674698+    6   DOS 16-bit>32M
```

Now, how do you find the new values sought for **fdisk**? In the given example of the 4 GB hard disk with 64 heads, 32 sectors and 4095 cylinders stated by **fdisk** the resultant total capacity is 64*32*4095*512 bytes = 4095 MB. Where there are 512 Bytes per sector. *Calculating the actual values*

If you now assume the number of heads is 255 and the number of sectors id 63 then the following equation results: 255*63*cylinders*512 Bytes = 4095 MB. You can see from the error messages in the partition table above that this assumption seems to be right. *An equation with one unknown*

Solving this equation for cylinders gives 522 cylinders. These new values now have to be entered in **fdisk**. To do this you have to change to the expert mode of **fdisk** with the **x** command and enter the new parameters for the heads, sectors, and cylinders. *Entering the new cylinder values*

In the expert mode you can do this with the commands **c** (cylinders), **h** (heads) and **s** (sectors). Due to the calculation above there are 255 heads and 63 sectors. Please never enter 256 heads, if you want to use DOS. A head count of 256 causes DOS to crash without comment. So, enter the new values: *Never enter 256 heads!*

```
Expert command (m for help): h
Number of heads (1-256): 255

Expert command (m for help): s
Number of sectors (1-63): 63
Warning: setting sector offset for DOS compatibility

Expert command (m for help): c
Number of cylinders (1-65535): 522
```

After having entered these values in the expert mode of **fdisk**, return to the normal main menu of **fdisk** with the **r** command. Now all the warnings should disappear thus indicating that you have found the right values: *Error messages disappear*

```
Command (m for help): p
Disk /dev/sda: 255 heads, 63 sectors, 522 cylinders
Units = cylinders of 16065 * 512 bytes

Device  Boot  Begin  Start   End  Blocks    Id  System
/dev/sda1          1      1    96  771088+    6  DOS 16-bit>32M
/dev/sda2     *   97     97   249 1228972+   82  Linux swap
/dev/sda3        250    250   313  514080    a5  BSD/386
/dev/sda4        314    314   522 1678792+    5  Extended
/dev/sda5        314    314   345  257008+   83  Linux native
/dev/sda6        346    346   353   64228+   83  Linux native
/dev/sda7        354    354   438  682731     6  DOS 16-bit>32M
/dev/sda8        439    439   522  674698+    6  DOS 16-bit>32M
```

*Error messages
have to disappear*

If the error messages haven't disappeared, you haven't found out the right values yet. Repeat the process of entering new values until the error messages have disappeared and don't forget to make a note of these values in your hardware documents.

*Entering correct
values for each use*

After having entered the correct values in the expert mode, you can continue your work with **fdisk**. Note that you unfortunately have to enter the values in the expert mode each time **fdisk** is run, as the values are not stored permanently.

/etc/disktab

If you also want to use **lilo**, in order to be able to boot Linux directly from the hard disk, you still have to determine the right entries for the **/etc/disktab** file. You will obtain them when changing the **fdisk** display of the partitioning from units to sectors with **u**. These sector options correspond to the blocks of the LBA mode.

```
Command (m for help): u
Changing display/entry units to sectors
```

Then ask again for an output of the partition table:

```
Command (m for help): p

Disk /dev/sda: 255 heads, 63 sectors, 522 cylinders
Units = sectors of 1 * 512 bytes

Device Boot     Begin    Start      End  Blocks    Id System
/dev/sda1          63       63  1542239  771088+    6 DOS 16-bit>32M
/dev/sda2     * 1542240  1542240  4000184 1228972+  82 Linux swap
/dev/sda3     4000185  4000185  5028344  514080    a5 BSD/386
/dev/sda4     5028345  5028345  8385929 1678792+    5 Extended
/dev/sda5     5028408  5028408  5542424  257008+   83 Linux native
/dev/sda6     5542488  5542488  5670944   64228+   83 Linux native
/dev/sda7     5671008  5671008  7036469  682731     6 DOS 16-bit>32M
/dev/sda8     7036533  7036533  8385929  674698+    6 DOS 16-bit>32M
```

*Option with
sector numbers*

You will see that the start, size, and end of the partitions are no longer stated in cylinders, but in sectors (which are used by Linux for the access on the hard disk). Now enter these sector values in the **/etc/disktab** file. In our example, the entries of this file should look like this:

# Dev.	BIOS	Secs/	Heads/	Cylin-	Part.		
# num.	code	track	cylin.	ders	offset		
0x801	0x80	63	255	522	63	#	/dev/sda1
0x802	0x80	63	255	522	1542240	#	/dev/sda2
0x803	0x80	63	255	522	4000185	#	/dev/sda3
0x805	0x80	63	255	522	5028408	#	/dev/sda5
0x806	0x80	63	255	522	5542488	#	/dev/sda6
0x807	0x80	63	255	522	5671008	#	/dev/sda7
0x808	0x80	63	255	522	7036533	#	/dev/sda8

Let's hope that this procedure wasn't too confusing for you. We cannot assure you that this method leads to the desired result for every controller. In principle, though, the procedure should have been clarified by this example.

Do not be deterred

6.9   Compiling the Kernel

You should really try to compile a kernel configured specially for the system, if only to get experience with kernel generation. Experience shows that this procedure is much easier than most people suppose.

Especially adapted kernel

The sources for the system kernel will be found in the installed system under the path **/usr/src/linux**. An appropriate README explaining the process of a kernel configuration and generation in detail will also be located there. If you keep to the instructions stated there, you will have no problem compiling your own kernel.

Kernel sources under /usr/src/linux

Before you compile a new kernel, you should use any patches from LST for the original kernel sources by running the **mkpatch-2.0.***-script located under **/usr/src/patches/kernel**. The procedure necessary for this is explained in the file **/usr/src/linux/README.1st22**.

Do not forget the LST patches

To generate the new kernel then, the following simple steps are required:

- Change to the directory **/usr/src/linux**,

- run the command

    make config

    to determine which drivers should be contained in the kernel and which drivers should be available as loadable modules. If there are uncertainties about an option, there will be help at your disposal.

    make config

- With the command

    make depend

make depend

you prepare the kernel sources for the compiling, by checking and determining all dependencies. Do not interfere at this point. The time needed will be roughly 5 minutes.

- The command

  make zImage

make zImage

finally translates the new kernel from the kernel sources. You shouldn't interfere here either. The procedure lasts between 10 and 60 minutes depending on the computer.

rdev

- With the command

  rdev -R arch/i386/boot/zImage 1

Readonly flag

set the readonly flag for the boot process. The right root partition should be set automatically.

Shifting the kernel
to /boot

- Move the kernel under **arch/i386/boot** to **/** or to **/boot**, and rename it for example in **zImage-2.0.x**.

Do not forget to
call up LILO

- Enter the new kernel in **/etc/lilo.conf**, and then run the program **lilo** to register the new kernel with the bootloader.

Determining
drivers for
the kernel

The command **make config** runs a script with which you can determine the configuration of the new Linux kernel. As the script runs you will be asked about a number of drivers and options for the kernel. These can be set individually.

Help for the
kernel options

If you need further help on a certain item, an additional help text can be called up for every single entry. It is important to only choose the drivers which are necessary for your existing hardware. Each driver which isn't needed enlarges the kernel unnecessarily and negatively influences the boot behaviour.

Installing the
kernel sources

If you do not yet have the kernel source directory **/usr/src/ linux/**, you have to install the software package **linux-source- 2.0.*-1.i386.rpm** from the developer series. You also need the GNU C compiler **gcc** with the associated ancilliary programs from the developer series, in order to be able to generate your own kernel.

Kernel
configuration
with LISA

From the LISA version 2.0 on you will most probably be able to carry out the generation of a custom kernel just with LISA. Look under the menu "system configuration" in "system settings ..." for the item "system kernel". LISA carries out exactly the aforementioned commands, allows comfortable selection of the desired kernel options and afterwards installs the new kernel with **lilo** for your system.

Keeping the old
kernel to be on
the safe side

To be on the safe side, the kernel with which you have already booted successfully should be left in the LILO boot menu as an option. If a mistake occurs during or after generating the new kernel and the system then cannot be started with the new kernel, you still can resort to the old kernel.

Networks

As much potential as Linux may have on a single computer, this operating system only develops its abilities to the full, when networking several computers.

Numerous possibilities for use are presented as soon as one links the computer to the world wide internet. With a quick enough connection one can not only send e-mail to any place desired or load files from any internet server, but also negotiate via video conference with business partners in Tokyo and New York.

Communication without limitations and regardless of distance

Besides web surfing, home banking, or teleshopping, the internet will also make it possible to choose your place of work. So, most of the time you could work at home with your Linux system, independent from your company headquarters, and need only connect to your employer's computers via an ISDN or other telephone line from time to time.

Independency from the central office

To the user, a network presents itself as homogeneous construction, a kind of "black box", through which the communication takes place. The network is accessed by uniform mechanisms and always behaves in the same manner, with the exception of varying response times and transfer rates. It doesn't make any difference whether you communicate with the ends of the world or with the computer next to you.

Network as black box

Above all we want to give you an overview and some insight into the sometimes very complicated world of networks. Details of administration would go far beyond the scope of this book. So instead, in the last chapter, we give you some pointers to documentation available online in your system.

Complex network world

As network administrator you have to make sure that the complexity of the underlying network stays hidden to the user to the greatest possible extent. This implies the configuration of the network connection, e.g. for a local ethernet, and of the above mentioned network services, such as Mail, News or FTP.

Hiding the complexity

Under DOS or Windows you must first of all load special drivers and install additional software for getting a connection to a network. Sometimes each application even needs its own driver or special support.

Special drivers

139

Network ability is completely integrated

The basic networking ability of Linux is already complete and directly integrated in the operating system in a very fundamental way. Aside from better efficiency, this has the advantage that all applications can draw directly on the networking capability. Furthermore, much less storage is needed and the operating system automatically administers the network resources.

Basic understanding

We tried to write this chapter in such a way that you will be able to answer the necessary questions on the configuration asked by LISA, without having an in depth knowledge of networks. Our experience with customer support has shown that many users have no understanding of the basic concepts. This is not suprising as it is a complex topic and an area in which relatively few people have had the opportunity to gather experience.

Right information on LISA

Without a basic familiarity it can be very difficult, to carry out a network configuration without making mistakes. By just using the try and see method, one unfortunately won't get very far. With the LISA network connection for installation we want you to get a feeling for what should be taken into account for the network configuration, so that you can cope better with its demands.

7.1 Network Types and Protocols

Purpose

When connecting several computers via network they are refered to according to their purpose.

- A host is a computer that only uses the services of the network; this is called end system.

- A router is a computer in the network, which passes on information from one part of a network to another, or determines their route. It can also be called an intermediate in the system.

- Both types, host and router, are described as a system.

Network types

When connecting computers there are several types of networks which differ from each other in the hardware used. Linux supports almost all common network types, so that it is mostly no problem to connect Linux to an existing network. Amongst others, following network types are supported:

- ethernet with a transfer rate of 10 and 100 MBit/s;

- SMB (Session Message Block) based networks, like for example Windows for Workgroups, Windows 95 or OS/2 LAN-Manager;

- Novell Netware, with special connection to the Caldera Network Desktop;

- IBM Token Ring, also widespread alongside ethernet;

- Appletalk;

- ATM (Asynchronous Transfer Mode);

- ISDN (Integrated Services Digital Network);

- AX.25 (amateur radio broadcasts);

- Arcnet, for which there exist cheap network cards.

The exchange of data within these networks is carried out with several protocols which determine the language, so to speak, between *Network protocols* the systems. For this too, Linux offers support for everything with standing and reputation:

- TCP/IP (Transmission Control Protocol / Internet Protocol) – the standard protocol in the Unix world;

- UUCP (Unix to Unix Copy) – a somewhat older protocol, which has mainly been used for connections via modem;

- FIDO – an individual network, which doesn't depend on a certain operating system and is also based on modem connections;

- ISDN protocols for national and Euro ISDN;

- SLIP (Serial Line Internet Protocol) – makes IP possible via a serial line;

- PPP (Point to Point Protocol) – successor to SLIP;

- PLIP (Parallel Line Internet Protocol), makes IP possible via a parallel interface;

- SMB (Session Message Block) – the protocol for the Windows world, which can be accessed under Linux via SAMBA.

A variety of different network application programs (services) are *Network services* based on the TCP/IP protocol:

- the World Wide Web (WWW) – the most popular representative of all network services which, as one can easily see by the name, represents a world wide information system.

- electronic mail (e-mail) – the most convenient and the quickest way for sending letters and information to any place in the world within seconds;

- black boards (Net News) – where everyone can search for or leave information on particular topics;

- online chats (IRC or Talk) with other users of the network;

- working sessions on and data transfer to remoted computers of the network;

- network filesystems – via which you have access to data of remote computers, as if these were in your local filesystem;

- various information services allowing access to network wide data.

service programs   Most of these services are provided with a number of programs which make these services usable:

- **netscape**, **Mosaic**, **chimera** or **arena** make it possible to surf the World Wide Web;

- **mail**, **elm** and **pine** make it possible to read and write e-mails;

- **sendmail** and **smail** send and deliver e-mails;

- **nn**, **tin**, **trn** or **xnews** can be used for reading and writing net news;

- **inn** or **cnews** provide you with these net news in your system;

- **talk** or **irc** make it possible to have real time communication with other network users;

- **telnet**, **rlogin** and **rsh** make it possible to have working sessions on remote computers;

- **ftp** and **rcp** make it possible to transfer data to and from remoted computers;

- **nfsd**, **mountd** and **amd** make it possible to export or include filesystems via the network;

- **finger**, **archie** or **gopher** make it possible to ask for special information.

7.2 The OSI Reference Model

To understand better how the exchange of information in the network functions, one has to know that it is divided into several layers. The OSI/ISO layer model is the most suitable for this purpose (Fig. 7.1).

Layer model

With the layer model the ISO[1] has created OSI[2], the foundation for communication between different (open) systems. This model determines the communication relationships in hierarchically arranged layers, also often called levels.

International standardization

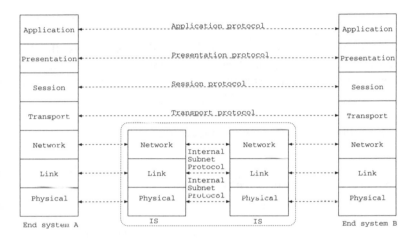

Fig. 7.1: The OSI reference model.

On the whole there are seven layers, which extend from a low level, the hardware, to the application programs at the highest layer. The communication exchange between the layers takes place from two different perspectives:

Seven layers

- the logical information exchange between two instances of the same layer in different end systems works via protocols, that means their common language, and

- the actual information exchange between the upper and the lower adjacent layers in the same system via defined interfaces, that is the services between the layers.

Figure 7.2 shows the logical information exchange horizontally and the physical exchange vertically. The services of a level are called up via Service Access Points (SAP).

Information exchange

[1] International Standardization Organisation
[2] Open System Interconnection

The information exchange via the layers of the OSI model happens absolutely transparently, so that the user will not notice. If you are aware of this principle, some processes will be much easier to understand.

Transparent communication

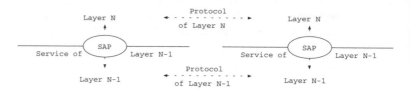

Fig. 7.2: Logical and physical flow of information in the OSI model.

Now we want to introduce you to some of the seven levels of the OSI model. We will restrict ourselves, though, to the those essential aspects which are meaningful in practical terms.

7.2.1 Layer 1 – The Physical Connection

Bit transfer layer

The first or lower layer is the bit transfer layer (physical layer). It is a physical connection between two systems. It can consist of different connection types, topologies and media as well as the respective protocols.

Connection type

The connection type states when and how long the connection will be made. One differentiates between the following connection types:

- permanent connection, which is continuously available, often called "online";

- dynamic connection, the semipermanent connection (SPC), where the connection is created on demand (e.g. via a telephone line, as soon as a request to a remote computer is made);

- staged connection, where the accumulated data are stored until there is a connection to the addressee. Connections are often made at fixed times e.g. at night. This principle is primarily used for UUCP and FIDO. The retrival of data is called polling.

Network topology

The topology of a net, that is the structure in which the single computers of the net are connected, is defined accordingly:

- point to point connection, with which two systems are always connected,

- connection via a common bus, which each single system is linked to,

- loop connection, which corresponds to a closed bus,

- intermeshed connection, which is a combination of the aforementioned connection types.

Physically, the data are transferred via a medium, such as a cable, *Physical transfer*
fibre optic cable or by radio. With the media there is usually a certain
protocol for the transfer. One differentiates between a:

- serial cable with two conductors (e.g. used for SLIP) – only point
  to point connections,

- parallel cable with eight conductors (e.g. used for PLIP) – only
  point to point connections,

- ethernet – coaxial cable with bus structure,

- twisted pair – in principle a twisted pair cable, only for point to
  point connections,

- Token Ring – also a coaxial cable with loop structure,

- FDDI (Fiber Distributed Digital Interface) – optical fibre cable
  with loop structure,

- ISDN   telephone line for point to point connection,

- radio transfer of the data via radiowaves with various structure
  possibilities.

Directly above the physical layer is the data link layer, the main
task of which is to guarantee faultless data transfer. This is achieved by *Ensuring a*
adding control information that is used to determine if faults occurred *faultless transfer*
during data transfer and then to a certain extent automatically correct
mistakes.

If it doesn't succeed in correcting mistakes, it will repeat the request
for the damaged data package from layer 1, until it has been transferred *Renewed demand*
correctly. Layer 3 can assume then that the data it recieves from layer 2
really have been transferred correctly.

7.2.2   Layer 3 – the communication

The communication layer, layer 3, usually provides the layer above it *Types of connection*
with two different network services:

- the link-orientated service,

- the linkless service

*Telephone works
link-orientated*

An example for a link-orientated service is the telephone. After the connection has been made (Dialling and receiving the call), a steady connection is provided to the subscribers for the duration of the service.

*Parcel is sent
linkless*

An example for a linkless service is the sending of a parcel. Neither the way taken by the parcel, nor the order of the arrival is ensured, when sending several packages simultaneously. One can only say that the parcel will hopefully arrive at the recipient.

Layer 3 is still carried out within the corresponding computer, whereas layer 4 is already independent from a particular computer and is therefore the first layer independent of the network type.

7.2.3 Layer 4 – Transport Layer

*Core of the
protocol hierarchy*

Layer 4, the transport layer, is the core of the whole protocol hierarchy. It is responsible for the data transport from the sender to the recipient as well as for a number of service quality parameters like the transfer rate or the probability of connection failure.

Routing

It determines the routing, that is which route in the network is taken by the data, and it ensures, that packages are neither lost on their way through the network, nor delivered in the wrong order.

*User-orientated
services*

The layers 5, 6 and 7, the session, presentation, and application layers, deal with the supply of user orientated services. They are able to use the bare fault free transport channel provided by layer 4.

Sessions

The session layer provides connections or sessions between applications and ensures that connections are made and finished. The presentation layer takes over conversion of data when the recipient and the sender consist of different hardware systems using different data representations.

7.2.4 Layer 7 – The Application Connection

Application layer

Layer 7, the application layer, is finally the layer on which common application programs start. That means it is the only layer you directly have to deal with. The lower layers perform their services transparently in the background.

*Network
applications*

Now we will turn to the practical part, the applications, which use the services of the layer model. Under Linux there is a great variety of these applications. The most important are:

- telnet, with which it is possible to have a working session on a remote computer;

- File Transmission Protocol (FTP), which allows the data transfer to and from a remote computer;

- mail, to exchange electronic mail;

- News, for providing us with the net news (i.e. information bulletin boards);

- World Wide Web (WWW), which makes it possible to retrieve or provide formatted graphical information;

- Archie, an information service, with which certain information within the network can be found;

- Gopher, also an information service allowing access to databases of various documents, data, and information;

- Finger, retrieves information about a known user on a remote computer;

- Talk, enabling live communication with another user in the network via screen and keyboard. A typed phone call, so to speak;

- Internet Relay Chat (IRC) corresponds to the Talk service, with the difference that many people can participate;

- Network Information Service (NIS) provides certain information network-wide, so that these mustn't be located on each computer of the network.

7.2.5 IP addresses and network classes

Before diving into practice, we should explain the meaning of the term IP address first. In principle, each IP address should be unique world-wide, that means, with just the IP address one can find the respective computer in the internet, if it exists at all.

Unambiguous IP addresses

An IP address consists of four bytes and is written in the form **a.b.c.d**, whereby you have to enter the respective values from 0 to 255 for **a** to **d**. So, **192.168.2.1** for example is a valid IP address.

Structure of an IP address

As far as the figures go, the result is more than 4 billion (256^4) different addresses. Inspite of this, they are running out because the IP addresses are not assigned singly, but rather addresses are always assigned in blocks for subnets. Within these networks, which are always reserved for a certain organisation or company, not every IP address is really used.

As far as the figures go, there are more than 4 billion IP addresses

There are five different types of networks, each of which contain a different number of IP addresses. The network classes which are most important for you are the following three:

Three different network classes

147

- A-class networks, which use the last three bytes for the individual computers. So each class A network may include more than 16 million IP addresses.

- B-class networks, which use the last two bytes for the computers of the network. They include more than 65,000 single IP addresses.

- C-class networks, where only the last byte is used for the single computers. Each class C network includes 256 separate IP addresses.

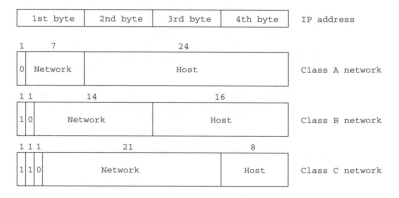

Fig. 7.3: The various network classes.

Fig. 7.3 shows the scheme. From there you can see the maximum number of different networks for each class:

- roughly 120 A-class networks worldwide,

- roughly 32,000 B-class networks worldwide,

- roughly 8 million C-class networks worldwide.

We are running short of IP addresses

As, meanwhile, there are more than 30 million internet users worldwide and many network classes and IP addresses are reserved "in a stock", one can easily understand why the free IP addresses are running out.[3]

First byte gives information on the network class

But how exactly are the IP address and network class classified? One can make a distinction by examining the first byte. Each value smaller than 128 stands for an A-class network, each value between 128 and

---

[3] The next version of the IP protocol will use 16 byte address information, which results in a huge number of IP addresses. This should be enough for our small planet, even if each toaster and each automobile gets its own IP address, the way it is planned.

191 for a B-class network, and each value from 192 to 223 stands for a C-class network.

IP addresses with a value larger than 223 (also called class D addresses) are addresses reserved for multicasting, which have no further significance for you at the moment.

Multicasting

7.2.6 Domain Name Service

Closely connected to the IP addresses are the associated domain names administered by DNS (Domain Name Service) servers. DNS is a distributed service. That means the information on the network is not complete on one single server, but is spread over many different servers.

Domain names

If a DNS server cannot resolve a special inquiry, it knows at least to which DNS server the inquiry can be forwarded, until a server has been found which is able to resolve the inquiry.

Resolving an inquiry

Thereby the FQHN (Fully Qualified Hostname) is resolved into the respective IP address. The name pattern of DNS is hierarchically constructed, as shown in Fig. 7.4.

Fully Qualified Hostname

A FQNH is always stated in the form **host.domain.top-leveldomain**, e.g. **peanut.nuts.com**.

You may be familiar with the top level domains **.de** for Deutschland (Germany), **.com** for commercial or **.edu** for education.

Top Level domain

Besides these there is **.mil** for military institutions, **.gov** for government institutions and **.org** for non-profit organisations. For the following examples we want to use the top level domain **.de**.

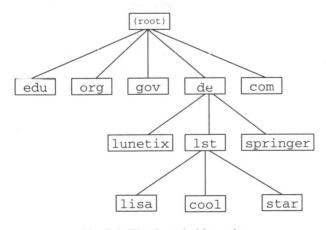

Fig. 7.4: The domain hierarchy.

The domain name put before the top level domain most often reflects the company or the organisation, like for example **springer.de**,

Domain name

lst.de or **lunetix.de**. For the next examples we will use **my-domain** as domain names.

The FQHN will be finally completed with the computer or host name, e.g. **peanuts.springer.de**, **lisa.lst.de** or **scotty.lunetix.de**. But these are just examples. You should not use these domain names for your computer, but rather use the domain that your internet provider or network administrator supplies.

Computer host name

Note that the hierarchical structure of the domain names and the division of the IP addresses are completely independent from each other. That means you can neither infer with certainty the respective IP address from certain domain names nor vice versa.

Domain names are independent from the IP addresses

Although within a sub-domain contiguous IP addresses are usually used in practice, it is possible that one or more of the IP addresses in the block are assigned to a completely different sub-domain.

7.3 Network Configuration in Practice

As now you will have knowledge on IP addresses and DNS too, it is high time to examine the practical aspects of networking.

Each computer within a network, running under Linux or Unix, runs the services listed above. This will be the case even if you reinstate your old 386 from the cellar, install Linux on it and network it with your workstation. It will also be the case if you are temporarily or continuously linked to the internet.

Network services available in standard models

If the latter will be the case, then be aware of the fact that a great number of these services can not only be used from your computer to other computers linked to the internet, but also vice versa. That means that, as soon as you are online, it is at any time possible that someone external logs in on your computer or calls up data from your computer.

Services most often possible in both directions

With POWER LINUX though, we attached importance to creating an outwardly safe system. So, no root login from outside will be possible since the shadow password system is used, network connections are supervised by the TCP wrapper, filesystems are exported with the **root-squash** option via NFS, and all important system events are logged in detail.

Attached importance to security

Most probably you will understand now, why we urged you to distribute passwords, safe ones that is, to the users. If there are users in your system who have no password, it can theoretically happen that someone external gets hold of information on the users of your system. Then he or she can log in on your computer and either do harm or steal information.

Danger from outside

As long as you are temporarily connected to the internet, you might recognise such actions, as you yourself are logged into your system and so you can react to attempts to log in from outside.

If you have a permanent internet connection via a permanent line, you have to see to it that the computer is safe even if you are not working on it. Especially at night, a hacker could obtain access to your system unnoticed and do what ever he or she wants without being disturbed.

Protecting against hackers

You must have knowledge of which network services are offered by your system and how to set them up for the utmost security. But before we get to grips with high level network administration, we will first of all start with the basics.

Making services safe

After having given you a lot of theory in the last section (please forgive us, but it is a matter of fact that computer scientists are followed by this shadow for a lifetime) we will explain which steps are necessary for you to connect your computer to other computers and other networks.

Enough theory!

You have the choice between two different methods for this. You can either use LISA for the network connection or do the necessary steps by hand.

LISA or making by hand?

We want to start with the more simple case, namely with connecting using LISA. Then we want to explain which steps are carried out by LISA. If you carry them out by hand you will get the same result.

Connecting with LISA

While installing, you have already been asked for the network connection. If you have chosen installation via NFS, the most important questions for the network connection have been asked already, having chosen the installation source.

Essential details already when installing NFS

The questions will occur anyway within the framework of the system configuration. Therefore, we want to give a short explanation on the background to the questions and how you can answer them.

First of all you will be asked whether or not you want to use the network. But of course!

Now you need a number of details on how to use the network:

- the network interface, that is the interface via which you are connected with the world outside,

- the name for this interface (FQHN), under which the computer can be addressed,

- the IP address for this interface, that is the numerical address under which this interface is unambiguously known worldwide,

- the network mask, which determines the type and size of your network,

- the broadcast address, which determines to which computer group you can send your broadcast messages and through this determine which further IP addresses belong to your network,

- the Default Router, that is the computer which connects you to the internet or which is responsible for determining the routes within your local network.

We will clarify the necessary details with some examples. The IP addresses from the area **192.168.2.x** have the peculiarity that they are not routed world wide, that is that they cannot be used within the internet. They serve instead as test subjects.

Special IP addresses for testing

While you should always just use IP addresses, which are allocated to you by your internet provider or especially network administrator, these test addresses can be used without any risk for test purposes. But it doesn't make sense to use them for a connection to the internet.

Using allocated IP addresses only

There are several possibilities for getting in contact with the world outside with your computer via TCP/IP the standard internet protocol. The most common types of connection are:

connection via TCP/IP

- via the serial interface with SLIP or PPP or via the parallel interface with PLIP,

- via a network card, which will most probably be an ethernet card.

So, first state the interface to be used for network interfaces. If you operate an ethernet card in your computer, then the network interface will usually be **eth0**.

Ethernet interface eth0

Whereas, if the computer should function as router with several ethernet cards, the further network cards are numbered through in order, that means **eth0** for the first ethernet card, **eth1** for the second ethernet card and so on.

Router

The router distinguishes itself by being connected to the local net via a network interface and to an external network or the internet via a second interface. These two network interfaces will then have different IP addresses.

Two network interfaces

Of course, the serial interface can also serve as second network interface for a router. In this case, for the second interface state the corresponding interface name of PPP or SLIP.

PPP as second network connection

If you want to carry out the network connection via PPP, then use, depending on how the serial interfaces have been configured, the interface **ppp0**, **ppp1** or **ppp2**.

Interface ppp0

If using SLIP, the interfaces are **sl0**, **sl1** and **sl2** and if you use PLIP, the interfaces are called **plip0**, **plip1** and **plip2**, depending on which interface is used.

Interface sl0 and plip0

Now you have to state a name for this interface. You should always use a FQHN (see Sect. 7.2.6) here, as this interface can be addressed under an unambigous name.

FQHN

You can see which interfaces exist from the LISA system analysis or by displaying them with the command **cat /proc/net/dev**.

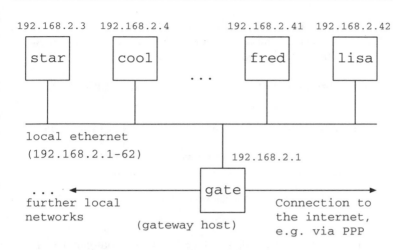

Fig. 7.5: An example network.

Now each interface must get an IP address. Figure 7.5 shows *Example network*
an example network. From this we will use the computers **lisa.my-**
domain.de and **gate.mydomain.de** for the following examples.
The computer **lisa** gets the IP address **192.168.2.42**.

Besides the IP address, also the broadcast and netmask addresses
have to be set for an interface. For example, if you have a C-class *Broadcast address*
network, this corresponds to the network mask **255.255.255.0**. To *and network mask*
give an example, we have subdivided it into four subnets, thereby two
additional bits of the address are used for the network masking and thus
result in the network mask **255.255.255.192**.

The broadcast address ensues from setting all the host bits of the *Calculating the*
IP addresses to **1**. In this case we get **192.168.2.63**. The network *broadcast address*
address results from setting all host bits of the IP addresses to **0**. This
gives **192.168.2.0**.

Now the interface can be configured and a route for the subnet can be
entered. If you have chosen a point to point connection for the network *Address of the*
installation, like for example PLIP or PPP, you have to state the address *PPP server*
of the counterpart of your point to point connection, that is the address
of the PPP server used. Then you will be asked which default router is
used, that is the computer that links you to the world outside. In our *Default router*
example it will be the computer **gate.mydomain.de**.

Note that the IP address for the interface of your router has to be
located within the subnet. We will use **192.168.2.1** now as IP *Address within*
address for the interface of **gate.yourdomain.de**. It is common *the subnet*
practice, but not necessary, to choose either the smallest possible or the
greatest possible IP address of the subnet for the router.

Now let's have a look at the steps, which will be carried out by LISA, if you do the configuration above. A number of basic commands are used, which address and configure the network interface:

- **ifconfig** (interface configuration), for configuring the network interface,

- **route** and **traceroute**, to set and check network routing,

- **ping**, to "ping" other computers of the network, that means to addess them breifly to see if they are answering,

- **netstat**, to get information on the status and condition of the network.

Ifconfig

First of all the network interface has to be configured with the **ifconfig** command. In our example this is carried out by the following command:

```
ifconfig eth0 192.168.2.42 netmask 255.255.255.192
broadcast 192.168.2.63
```

The general call syntax of the command **ifconfig** goes as follows:

```
ifconfig INTERFACE IPADDR netmask NETMSK broadcast BRDCST
```

or for point to point connections

```
ifconfig INTERFACE IPADDR pointopoint IPADDR
```

If, after having run **ifconfig**, you receive an error message like

```
eth0: unknown interface
```

Cause of the fault

then no interface card named **eth0**, could be found. This will be the case for example, if your ethernet card hasn't been recognised, isn't supported or if you haven't loaded the required driver.

Routing with route

After the initialisation of the network interface with **ifconfig** the route for the right routing has to be set:

```
route add -net 192.168.2.0
```

Default route

Then a default route has to be set. For this the **route** command is used again:

```
route add default gw 192.168.2.1
```

The general call syntax of the **route** command goes as follows:

```
route add [-net|-host] ROUTEADDR [gw GATEWAYADDR]
```

or

```
route add default gw GATEWAYADDR
```

The **default** option is always a synonym for **0.0.0.0**. Besides
the route, LISA enters the name which you have allocated for this interface in the file **/etc/hosts**. This is important, as you can not draw *Host table*
upon any named server at this point in time and therefore the conversion */etc/hosts*
of computer names into IP addresses has to be carried out via the file
/etc/hosts.

Additionally, LISA enters the first network as **localnet** in the file *Entry in*
/etc/networks, in which all networks known to your computer are */etc/networks*
entered.

Each detail is also recorded in the central configuration file **/etc/** *Central*
system.cnf of LISA, for having it available after a reboot. Never *configuration file*
change the entries of **system.cnf** by hand, as otherwise inconsisten- *system.cnf*
cies could occur in the system.

7.3.1 Searching for Errors and Making a Diagnosis

It is the network configuration which very often causes problems. We
want to give you some clues as how to discover the mistakes.

The first step is to make a network diagnosis with LISA to find out *LISA network*
simple problems. The network diagnosis can be reached with the com- *diagnosis*
mand **lisa --netdiag**. You will get further help to the single menu
items via the online help.

If LISA cannot give you further help, you should try to check the
correct settings by hand with the respective commands.

With the **ifconfig -a** command all configured interfaces can be *Displaying all*
displayed and you can check whether the IP addresses and the broadcast *interfaces with*
and network masks have been set correctly. This can look as follows: *ifconfig -a*

```
root@lisa~# ifconfig -a

lo      Link encap:Local Loopback
        inet addr:127.0.0.1  Bcast:127.255.255.255
        Mask:255.0.0.0
        UP BROADCAST LOOPBACK RUNNING  MTU:3584  Metric:1
        RX packets:18 errors:0 dropped:0 overruns:0
        TX packets:18 errors:0 dropped:0 overruns:0

eth0    Link encap:10Mbps Ethernet HWaddr 00:A0:24:77:6C:7E
        inet addr:192.168.2.42  Bcast:192.168.2.63
        Mask:255.255.255.192
        UP BROADCAST RUNNING MULTICAST  MTU:1500  Metric:1
        RX packets:0 errors:0 dropped:0 overruns:0
        TX packets:0 errors:0 dropped:0 overruns:0
        Interrupt:11 Base address:0x300
```

155

*Construction
of the display*

Loopback device

*Displaying the
routing table*

In the first line you can see the name of the network interface. Besides the already clarified interface names **eth0**, **eth1** and **ppp0** there can also appear **lo** for the internal loopback device or **isdn0** for the first ISDN interface.

The loopback device **lo**, by the way, is continuously available and is always provided with the IP address **127.0.0.1**. All network services which you call up for this device, are refered to your local computer.

With the **route -n** command you can get the routing table. This could look as follows:

```
root@lisa~# route -n

Kernel routing table
Destination Gateway Genmask        Flags MSS Window Use Iface
192.168.2.0  *       255.255.255.192 U     1500 0      0 eth0
127.0.0.0    *       255.0.0.0       U     3584 0      0 lo
default      192.168.2.1 *          UG    1500 0      0 eth0
```

Net or host route?

It is important to differentiate between net and host routes. Host routes can be recognised by **UH** in the **Flags** column and stands for **Up** and **Host**. Net routes can be recognised by **U** and **UG**, where G stands for gateway.

In the display above, you can see that a net route is set to **127.0.0.0** the loopback interface; a net route **192.168.2.0** is set on the interface **eth0** and that the default route points to the gateway **192.168.2.1**.

Calling with ping

With the **ping** command[4] you can check whether or not certain computers of the network are available and responding. **ping** runs in a continous loop and, in the default setting, sends IP packages to the destined address every second.

*Recipient issues a
receipt for the
packages*

The destined address gives a receipt for these packages and sends them back. When the target computer answers, you will see the receipt of the answer packages every second. The **ping** command can be aborted at any time with **CTRL-C**.

*Starting with the
own address*

First of all start with the IP address of your network interface, in this case **192.168.2.42**. Then you will see an output which should look like:

```
root@lisa~# ping 192.168.2.42

PING 192.168.2.42 (192.168.2.42): 56 data bytes
64 bytes from 192.168.2.42: icmp_seq=0 ttl=64 time=0.4 ms
64 bytes from 192.168.2.42: icmp_seq=1 ttl=64 time=0.2 ms

--- lisa.mydomain.de ping statistics ---
2 packets transmitted, 2 packets received, 0% packet loss
round-trip min/avg/max = 0.2/0.3/0.4 ms
```

[4] Note that the **ping** command is located on the path for the superuser only. If you want to use it as a normal user, you must either start it with the absolute path **/sbin/ping** or add **/sbin** to your path.

Check then, whether your default router is answering, in this case
192.168.2.1:

*Answer from the
default router*

```
root@lisa~# ping 192.168.2.1

PING 192.168.2.1 (192.168.2.1): 56 data bytes
64 bytes from 192.168.2.1: icmp_seq=0 ttl=64 time=0.4 ms
64 bytes from 192.168.2.1: icmp_seq=1 ttl=64 time=0.2 ms

--- lisa.mydomain.de ping statistics ---
2 packets transmitted, 2 packets received, 0% packet loss
round-trip min/avg/max = 0.2/0.3/0.4 ms
```

Lastly check whether or not a computer located beyond your default
router can be accessed. For this you can for example use the IP address
131.188.44.111.

*Computer beyond
the default router*

If a counterpart doesn't answer, check whether the cables and the
terminations are in order and whether the network interfaces of
the computers involved have been configured correctly and whether
they are "up".

*Avoiding the cause
of the faults*

If you get an error message of the kind:

ping: sendto: Network is unreachable

the kernel with the existing routing table cannot determine where to
send the package, which means your routing table is incomplete. This
can be the case, for example, if you are only temporarily connected
with the internet per dialup and if there is no connection and therefore
no default route at the moment.

*Incomplete
routing table*

With the **traceroute** command[5] you can follow the route within
the network to a certain computer. It is possible that a connection doesn't
work because the the time for answering is longer than the stated time-
out value or the connection to your default router has some problems.

*Following the route
with traceroute*

traceroute shows the route of the connection by displaying each
single station on the route to the target computer, so that the route can
be checked and possible "bottle necks" can be discovered. These can
be recognised by the fact that, instead of the name of the computer on
the way to the target computer, there are three stars * displayed, which
indicates that there are greater time delays.

*Displaying the
single stations
of the route*

```
traceroute to trick.springer.de (192.129.24.12), 30 hops max, 40 byte packets
  1  isdn (193.98.158.65)  1.763ms  1.472ms  1.359ms
  2  skunk3-gw.unlisys.net (194.64.15.202)  33.55ms  56.882ms  39.068ms
  3  skunk3-xip.unlisys.net (194.64.15.201)  38.634ms  30.966ms  39.137ms
  4  ugate01.unlisys.net (194.64.15.65)  39.371ms  72.064ms  39.146ms
  5  berlin.core.xlink.net (193.141.43.221)  198.773ms  192.967ms  159.244ms
  6  karlsruhe.core.xlink.net (193.141.43.138)  237.824ms  153.123ms  238.455ms
  7  karlsruhe2.core.xlink.net (194.122.225.13)  158.088ms  73.052ms  79.159ms
  8  SPGW1.springer.DE (188.1.132.241)  358.667ms  264.504ms  279.06ms
  9  * * trick.ntp.springer.de (192.129.24.12)  298.848ms
```

---

[5] The **traceroute** command too, is not contained in the path of a normal user.
It is located under **/usr/sbin/**.

Short-term network
overload

The reason for this can lie in a short-term network overload. This means that within a stated interval, no feedback comes from the target computer. If you try to call up five minutes later, the way may be "free" again and the route to the target computer will be displayed without interruption.

Further Documentation

Hopefully we have given you a comprehensible introduction to Linux with this book. Although it is beyond the scope of this book to discuss every detail of Linux, there are still a number of sources which go a long way toward answering any remaining questions. There is not only a mass of online documentation in the system itself, but now there are also a number of good books on Linux.

There are always some questions that remain unanswered

8.1   Online Documentation

Though you will find a variety of documentation in your POWER LINUX system, it will not always be so easy to find the right documentation.

Finding the right documentation

8.1.1   System Documentation

The quickest and most effective source of information will usually be the manual page system. It doesn't matter if you work with **xman** or with **man** as, using the section overview of **xman**, the cross-references at the end of a manual page, or the assistance of the **apropos** command, one should always find the right manual page.

man, xman and apropos

Unfortunately, the Linux manual pages are not maintained as enthusiastically as the programs they describe. So you may often find that a manual page doesn't correctly describe the corresponding program.

Of good programmers and bad writers

If in doubt, assume that the command is better updated, and is more functional, than promised in the manual page. If this seems to be the case, compare the manual page with the command's **usage** message or glance at the source code of the command.

Comparing the usage messages

Besides the manual pages you will find a great part of the system documentation on certain programs or program packages in the directory **/usr/doc/package_name**.

The best and above all the most reliable source of information for the advanced user or programmer is naturally the source code. Even if you are not a programmer yet, you should appreciate the value of source code and become more familar with this topic. After all, it is a completely new situation, in that the complete source code for all parts of the system is available and is guaranteed to continue to be available in the future. The sources for programs already installed can be found in the directory **/usr/src/program_name**.

*Source code
under /usr/src*

While the documentation under **/usr/doc** will be automatically installed with each program package, the source code is always located in an own source code package (SRPM). Just install the corresponding **srpm** package, unpack it and you will find the source code under **/usr/src/redhat/BUILD**. See the RPM HOWTO for more details.

SRPM packages

8.2 HOWTOs and FAQs

*HOWTOs – the
setup recipes
for Linux*

The Linux HOWTOs are a kind of collection of single documents on specialized topics. They are mostly well up to date and are continually extented and improved. You can find them in the directory **/usr/doc/ HOWTO**.

*HOWTOs in
several formats*

The most commonly installed format is pure ASCII text, but often other formats like SGML, HTML or PostScript will be installed as well. The HOWTOs cover the whole Linux field. They go into frequently occuring problems in great detail and often offer several solutions for them.

*Basic
knowledge*

Even if you have no concrete problems, you can gain a lot of basic knowledge from the HOWTOs. The most imortant HOWTO documents for the start are for example:

- HOWTO-INDEX, the contents,
- BootPrompt-HOWTO, boot parameters for the kernel,
- Installation-HOWTO, help for the installation,
- Kernel-HOWTO, kernel versions and kernel generation,
- NET-2-HOWTO, Linux network code,
- PCI-HOWTO, Linux and PCI,
- PCMCIA-HOWTO, PCMCIA cards,
- Printing-HOWTO, printing and the printing system,
- SCSI-HOWTO, SCSI controller and devices,
- Tips-HOWTO, useful tips and tricks,
- UMSDOS-HOWTO, Linux within a DOS partition,
- XFree86-HOWTO, the XFree X Window system.

The FAQs (Frequently Asked Questions), which are most common in the internet, are in the case of Linux outnumbered by HOWTOs. Interesting FAQs are for example:

Frequently asked questions

- ATAPI-FAQ, ATAPI CD ROM drives,
- GCC-FAQ, the gcc C/C++/Objective-C Compiler,
- LILO-FAQ, the LILO bootloader,
- Linux-FAQ, general information on Linux,
- NET-FAQ, Linux in the network use,
- NFS-FAQ, the network filesystem,
- PPP-FAQ, connections with the point to point protocol,
- Wine-FAQ, the Windows emulator WINE.

8.3 The Linux Documentation Project

The Linux Documentation Project (LDP) started in the early beginnings of Linux development. The aim was to sufficiently document the system with various specialized books. These have been improved and extented during the course of time, and some can be bought in bookshops. You can find a list of the books in the directory **/usr/doc/LDP**, where they are mostly available in the PostScript format. We will give you some examples:

LDP – free documentation for a free system

- Installation & Getting Startet Guide by Matt Welsh,
- Kernel Hackers Guide by Michael K. Johnson,
- Network Administration Guide by Olaf Kirch,
- Programmers Guide by Sven Goldt et. al.,
- System Administrators Guide by Lars Wirzenius,
- Users Guide by Larry Greenfield.

8.4 World Wide Web

With a Web browser such as **arena** under X11 you can view the home-page for POWER LINUX . From there you can get a great proportion of the other documentation that has been converted to HTML format.

HTML documentation for's WWW

Unfortunately, distribution of the popular Web browsers **Netscape Navigator** and **Mosaic** on CD-ROM is not permitted. If you have access to the internet, you can download a version yourself for private use.

If you have access to the Internet, you can also have a look at our homepage at the address **http://www.1st.de**. There you can find out for example, if there are updates to download or if updates are in the pipeline. You can also checkout news on our current state of development and plans.

www.lst.de

8.5   Books on Linux

There has been such a boom in the publication of books on Linux that it will be difficult to find out which are the best. Therefore we will give you a short list, which we consider to be the most worthwhile reading.

Unix in a Nutshell

- "Unix in a Nutshell" by Daniel Gilly, published by the O'Reilly and Associates publishing house (ISBN 1-56592-001-5). This book is the classic Unix introduction and can be recommended to all readers who want to learn more on the basics of Unix. It can almost be applied to Linux without modification.

Network Administration

- "TCP/IP Network Administration" by Craig Hunt or the "Linux Network Administrator's Guide" by Olaf Kirch, both published by O'Reilly (ISBN 0-937175-82-X, 1-56592-087-2). These are the most suitable books for all prospective network specialists.

Linux Start-Up Guide

- "Linux Start-Up Guide" by Fred Hantelmann, part of the LINUX POWER PACK but also available separately (ISBN 3-540-62676-X). This book deals with the whole Linux system in detail.

Linux User's Handbook

- "The Linux User's Handbook" by Sebastian Hetze, Martin Mueller, Olaf Kirch and Dirk Hohndel (LunetIX Berlin, ISBN 3-929764-05-9). This was the first Linux book written in German and has become a real classic. Thanks to the great authors, it is very detailed and has much know-how on Linux. Unfortunately it's still only available in German.

Taking time for the bookshop

You should in any case take the time to drop in on your bookseller. You will find that there is a wide selection of books on Linux. You should first of all partly read the books worth considering, to be sure that you like the style and that the examples are comprehensible. There are also less suitable books which may put the beginner off as they are too detailed.

Great variety of Unix literature

By the way, you are not dependent on pure Linux books. Almost everything that can be found in a Unix book can also be applied to Linux.

It will be difficult without documentation

Without obtaining additional sources of help, it will be difficult for you to discover the real possibilities and advantages of Linux or Unix. Usually many of the good Unix ideas can only be understood from seeing an example, and then one doesn't have to reinvent the wheel every day.

Reference book

After all, you have made a start by reading this book, hopefully with joy. We hope that in the future it will remain useful to you as valuable reference book.

The Software Packages

So that you get a feeling of which software packages are included in POWER LINUX and what the packages contain we have made an alphabetical list of most of the software packages. You can also use this appendix as a quick reference to individual packages.

Alphabetical overview

The package descriptions are kept short intentionally as the list is intended as a quick overview. Note that the list is only representative of the situation at the time of writing and that the collection of packages changes continually with time.

Short package description

DEV: All necessary block and character devices for Linux.

ElectricFence: Development library for the kernel malloc debugger.

ImageMagick: Graphics package for displaying, converting and manipulating various image formats under X.

ImageMagick-devel: Static libraries and header files for development of graphical applications based on ImageMagick.

LPRng: Enhanced replacement for the standard UNIX printing tools.

LPRng-lpd: Enhanced UNIX print daemon compatible with the lpr standard.

LSM: The Linux Software Map.

LSTint: LST Power Linux International setup files.

NetKit-B: Various network programs.

SysVinit: System V compatible INIT program.

SysVinit-scripts: Scripts for System V init, such as 'inittab' and '/etc/rc.d'.

XFree86: XFree86 window system servers and fundamental programs.

XFree86-8514: XFree86 8514 server.

XFree86-AGX: XFree86 AGX server.

XFree86-I128: XFree86 I128 server.

XFree86-Mach32: XFree86 Mach32 server.

XFree86-Mach64: XFree86 Mach64 server.

XFree86-Mach8: XFree86 Mach8 server.

XFree86-Mono: XFree86 Mono server.

XFree86-P9000: XFree86 P9000 server.

XFree86-S3: XFree86 S3 server.

XFree86-S3V: XFree86 S3 ViRGE and ViRGE/VX server.

XFree86-SVGA: XFree86 SVGA server.

XFree86-VGA16: XFree86 VGA16 server.

XFree86-W32: XFree86 W32 server.

XFree86-Xnest: XFree86 nesting server.

XFree86-Xvfb: XFree86 Xvfb server.

XFree86-addons: X11R6 miscelleanous programs and their man pages.

XFree86-contrib: Additional programs for X11R6 from the 'contrib tapes'.

XFree86-devel: X11R6 static libraries, headers and programming man pages.

XFree86-develprof: X11R6 profiling libraries.

XFree86-develstatic: X11R6 static libraries.

XFree86-fonts: XFree86 Window System basic fonts.

XFree86-fonts100: X11R6 100dpi fonts.

XFree86-fonts75: X11R6 75dpi fonts.

XFree86-fontscyrillic: X11R6 cyrillic fonts – only need on server side.

XFree86-fontserver: X11R6 font server – only needed on server side.

XFree86-fontsextra: X11R6 hebrew and asiatic fonts – only needed on server side.

XFree86-fontsscale: X11R6 scalable fonts – only needed on server side.

XFree86-imake: X11R6 'imake' programming tools.

XFree86-misc: X11R6 miscelleanous programs and their man pages.

XFree86-programs: Additional programs for X11R6 from the 'contrib tapes'.

XFree86-server: XFree86 Window System server basic stuff.

XFree86-server-devel: XFree86 devel stuff for dga, misc, vidmode.

XFree86-server-modules: XFree86 loadable server modules for pex, xie, dga.

XFree86-setup: XFree86 setup program 'XF86Setup'.

XFree86-twm: Tab window manager for X.

XFree86-xdm: Display manager allowing the user to log in or out of the system under X.

XFree86-xsm: X session manager.

Xaw3d: The 3D Athena widget libraries version 1.3, which can replace the normal Athena widget library.

Xaw3d-devel: Header files and static libraries for developing programs that use Xaw3d.

Xconfigurator: X configuration utility.

abuse: Abuse – A really cool X/SVGA game.

acm: X based flight combat game.

adduser: User administration program.

adjtimex: User level frontend to adjtimex-syscall.

amd: The automounter which allows filesystems to be mounted on demand.

anonftp: Enables anonymous ftp access.

aout-libs: Libraries for compatibility with old a.out applications.

apache-docs: Documentation for the apache HTTP server.

apache-httpd: Apache HTTP server to provide WWW services.

archie: Information retrival system to query special archie databases containing entries from various FTP sites all over the net.

arena: Freely available, HTML-3 capable, WWW browser.

ash: Small bourne shell from Berkeley (only 40k).

at: The 'at' command allows processes to be started at a predetermined time.

aumix: Curses based audio mixer.

autoconf: Extendable package of GNU m4 macros which creates shell scripts to automatically configure source code packages. This package requires the GNU 'm4' package.

background: Additional background pictures for the X desktop.

bash: The GNU Bourne Again Shell which is functionally comparable to 'tcsh' and is the standard shell under Linux.

bc: GNU binary calculator with its own calculator language.

bdflush: The kernel daemon 'bdflush' is used to write altered data blocks in the cache back to the harddisk at regular intervals. This replaces the old update daemon.

bin86: The assembler 'as86', linker 'ld86', and GCC frontend 'bcc' from H.J. Lu.

bind: DNS name server used for name services in networks.

bind-devel: DNS resolver library and headers.

bind-doc: DNS documentation – Bind Operations Guide (BOG), RFC's and other.

bind-utils: DNS utilities, e.g. 'host', 'dig', 'dnsquery', 'nslookup'.

binutils: GNU binary development utilities.

bison: GNU parser generator (mighter than 'yacc').

blt: More widgets for the tk widget set.

blt-devel: Development libraries and header files for the BLT widgets.

bm2font: Bm2font converts bitmaps to LaTeX fonts.

bootp: Bootp/DHCP server that allows clients to automatically get their networking information.

bootpc: Bootpc, a client to get networking info from bootpd.

bsd-games: The BSD game collection contains classic games like 'backgammon', 'cribbage', 'fortune', 'hangman' and 'worms'.

buffer: Utility to speed up writing tapes on remote tape drives.

byacc: Public domain yacc parser generator.

cdp: Full screen text mode program for playing audio CD's.

cdwrite: Writes audio or data Compact Discs.

cmu-snmp: CMU Simple Network Management Protocol agent.

cmu-snmp-devel: CMU SNMP development libs and headers.

cmu-snmp-utils: CMU Simple Network Management Protocol utilities.

color-ls: Color ls – patched from GNU fileutils.

control-panel: Red Hat Control Panel.

coolmail: Shows status of the mailbox.

cpio: GNU 'cpio' archiving program (used by rpm).

cproto: C prototype utility.

crontabs: Root crontab file.

cvs: Concurrent version control system, a comprehensive frontend to 'rcs', the GNU revision control system. 'cvs' also operates on directory trees.

cxhextris: X based color version of hextris.

db: BSD database library for C.

db-devel: Development libraries and header files for the Berkeley database library.

ddd-doc: Motif based X interface to the GDB, DBX and XDB debuggers. Documentation and manual page.

ddd-dynamic: Motif based X interface to the GDB, DBX and XDB debuggers. Uses Motif 2.0 shared libraries.

ddd-semistatic: Motif based X interface to the GDB, DBX and XDB debuggers. With Motif 2.0 libraries statically linked in.

ddd-static: Motif based X interface to the GDB, DBX and XDB debuggers. Completely statically linked.

dialog: Tool to display tty dialog boxes from shell scripts.

diffutils: GNU 'diff' utilities differentiate files.

dip: Dip allows automatic modem dialing and creation of IP connections to be controlled with a script language.

dosemu: The experimental DOS emulator.

dump: BSD dump/restore backup system for extended-2 filesystems.

e2fsprogs: Programs and utilities for the extended-2 filesystem.

e2fsprogs-devel: Libraries and headers for the extended-2 filesystem tools.

easyedit: The 'easyedit' extension for Emacs.

ecc: Reed-Solomon Error Correcting Coder.

ed: GNU Line Editor 'ed', an 8-bit-clean POSIX line editor.

edy: Edy, a German coloured, window based editor.

efax: Sends and receives faxes over class 1 or class 2 modems.

eject: Ejects ejectable media and controls auto ejection.

elm: Menu based mail program 'elm'.

elvis: Elvis editor (Elvis is like VI).

exmh: 'exmh' mail program.

expect: A 'tcl' extension that allows easy interaction between programs and scripts.

expect-devel: The development and demo part of expect with man-pages.

ext2ed: Extended-2 filesystem editor (*for hackers only*).

f2c: Fortran to C convertor and static libraries.

f2c-libs: Shared libs for running dynamically linked fortran programs.

faces: Face saver database tools.

faces-devel: Face saver library and header.

faces-xface: Utilities to handle X-Face headers.

faq: FAQs – Frequently Asked Questions and answers about Linux.

fdutils: Low level floppy disk programs.

file: The GNU 'file' utility determines the type of any file with the help of '/etc/magic'.

fileutils: GNU File Utilities, a collection of many fundamental Unix programs.

findutils: GNU search utilities (find, xargs, and locate).

flex: GNU fast lexical analyzer generator.

flying: Pool, snooker, air hockey, and other table games.

fort77: A frontend driver for 'f2c'.

fortune-mod: Fortune cookie program with bug fixes.

free-lj4: Remote control tool for HP LJ4 printer series.

free-lj4-german: Remote control tool for HP LJ4 printer series in German.

fsstnd: Linux File System Standard documentation.

fstool: File system configuration tools.

ftptool: A nice ftp front end under Xview.

fvwm: Feeble (Fine?) Virtual Window Manager (incl. menus and configuration files).

fvwm-icons: Additional icons for the 'fvwm' window manager.

fvwm-modules: Additional modules for the fvwm window manager.

fwhois: A 'finger' style whois tool.

g77: GNU Fortran compiler 'g77'.

g77_lib: GNU Fortran 'g77' library

gawk: GNU 'awk' utility for manipulating patterns in text files.

gcal: Extended calendar with highlighting, holidays, etc.

gcc: GNU 'gcc' C compiler.

gcc-c++: C++ support for 'gcc'.

gcc-objc: Objective C support for 'gcc'.

gdb: GNU 'gdb', symbolic debugger for C and other languages.

gdbm: GNU database library for C.

gdbm-devel: Development libraries and header files for GNU database library.

gdbm-static: 'gdbm libraries for static linking.

gencat: 'gencat' message cataloging program (from NetBSD).

german-docs-L-Kurs: L-Kurs – An Introduction to Linux in German.

german-docs-intro: Linux documentation in German.

gettext: Utilties and libraries for programming with national language support (NLS).

getty_ps: Getty and uugetty programs for logging in.

ghostscript: PostScript interpreter and renderer.

ghostscript-fonts: Fonts for GhostScript.

ghostview: Ghostview user interface for ghostscript.

giftrans: Converts and manipulates GIFs.

gimp-static: General Image Manipulation Program, a Photoshop-like tool with many plug-ins.

git: GIT – GNU Interactive Tools.

glint: Graphical Linux INstallation Tool

gn: Gopher server.

gnat: GNU Ada compiler.

gnuchess: GNU 'chess' with 'xboard'. GNU Chess is a challenging ASCII based chess program and XBoard is its X interface.

gnuplot: 'gnuplot', an interactive tool for displaying values and functions.

gpm: General purpose mouse support for Linux.

gpm-devel: Development libraries and headers for writing mouse driven programs.

grep: GNU 'grep' utility.

groff: GNU 'groff' text formating utility.

groff-dvi: GNU 'groff' formatter for DVI.

groff-gxditview: GNU 'groff' formatter for preview under X.

groff-lj4: GNU 'groff' formatter for HP Laserjet 4 printers.

groff-misc: GNU 'groff' miscelleanous tools.

groff-ps: GNU 'groff' formatter for Postscript.

gzip: GNU 'gzip' compression utility version 1.2.4.

hdparm: Harddisk utility for reading and setting (E)IDE performance parameters.

helptool: Simple help file searching tool.

hman: Motif based manual browser under X.

howto-ascii: Linux HOWTOs – ASCII Text

howto-dvi: Linux HOWTOs in DVI format

howto-html: Linux HOWTOs in HTML format

howto-ps: Linux HOWTOs in Postscript format

howto-sgml: Linux HOWTOs in SGML format

html: Hyper text markup language 3.0 documentation in html format.

iBCS: Intel binary compliance standard (iBCS-2) module.

ical: Calender application based on Tcl/Tk.

illustrated-audio: Combined image and sound player for X.

imap: Provides support for IMAP and POP network mail protocols.

indent: GNU C indenting program for formatting C source code.

inn: 'internetnews' news transport system.

intimed: Time server for clock synchornization.

ipfwadm: IP firewall administration tool.

ipx: Utilites, init scripts, man pages and configuration files for IPX (Internetwork Packet Exchange – a Novell-centric datagram protocol).

ipxripd: IPX RIP/SAP daemon for discovering/advertising IPX routing information (RIP) and services (SAP) across an IPX internetwork.

ircii: Popular Unix Internet Relay Chat client.

ircii-help: Help files and documentation for ircii.

isdn4k-utils: Utilities for the kernel ISDN subsystem and some contributions.

ispell: GNU ispell – interactive spelling checker.

jed: Editor with multiple, keybindings, a c-like extension language, colors, and many other features.

jed-xjed: Jed editor for X.

joe: Joe, the easy to use editor.

kaffe: Kaffe is a freely available Java interpreter for many platforms and features a JIT-Engine (only for i386).

kbd: The loadable keyboard driver 'kbd'. Required for loading alternative keyboard layouts.

koules: A well written SVGAlib game.

kterm: Xterm with Kanji (japanese characters) support.

ktzset: Sets kernel time zone at boot time.

ld.so: 'ld.so' dynamic linker for shared libraries. With ancilliary programs. Contains 'ldconfig' and 'ldd' as well.

ldp-dvi: Linux Documentation Project in dvi format.

ldp-ps: Linux Documentation Project in postscript format.

ldp-txt: Linux Documentation Project in ascii format.

less: The pager 'less'.

lha: Creates and expands lharc format archives.

libc: libc and related libraries

libc-debug: libc with debugging information

libc-devel: Additional libraries required to compile

libc-profile: libc with profiling support

libc-pthreads: POSIX Threads Library.

libc-static: Libraries for static linking

libelf: Library for manipulating ELF object files.

libg++: GNU 'g++' library.

libg++-devel: Header files and libraries for C++ development.

libgnat: Ada run time system and shared library.

libgr: Graphics library set for fbm, jpeg, pbm, pgm, png, pnm, ppm, rle and tiff.

libgr-devel: Headers and static libraries for developing graphical applications.

libgr-progs: Utility programs for libgr.

libpam: PAM (pluggable authentication modules), a library for dynamic (re)configuration of user authentication methods like /etc/passwd, /etc/shadow, S/key and kerberos.

libpwdb: modular password database library

libtermcap: Library for accessing the termcap database.

libtermcap-devel: Development libraries and header files for termcap library.

libtiff-develdoc: Additional man pages for the functions in lib-tiff.

lilo: 'LILO', the boot loader for Linux and other operating systems from Werner Almesberger.

linux-kernel-binary: Linux kernel image and modules.

linux-kernel-doc: Linux kernel documentation.

linux-kernel-include: Linux kernel include files (required for C programming)

linux-source-alpha: Linux kernel sources for alpha axp architecture

linux-source-common: Linux kernel sources (architecture independent common sources).

linux-source-i386: Linux kernel sources for intel i386 architecture.

linux-source-m68k: Linux kernel sources for motorola m68k architecture.

linux-source-mips: Linux kernel sources for mips architecture.

linux-source-ppc: Linux kernel sources for power pc architecture

linux-source-sparc: Linux kernel sources for sparc architecture.

linuxdoc-sgml: Text formatting system used by the Linux Documentation Project.

lisa: The LISA utility from LST (Linux Installation and System Administration).

logrotate: Log file rotator.

losetup: Programs for setting up and configuring loopback devices.

lout: 'lout' text formatting system.

lout-doc: Full documentation for the 'lout' text formatting system.

lrzsz: Zmodem programs such as 'lzrz', 'sz', 'rz' and others.

lst-intl-html: LST information homepage in HTML.

lynx: Ascii based HTML browser.

lyx: A WYSIWYG frontend to LaTeX.

m4: GNU 'm4' macro processor.

macutils: Utilities for manipulating Macintosh file formats.

mailcap: Red Hat Mailcap package.

mailx: BSD 'mailx' mail program.

make: The GNU 'make' utility.

man-pages: System manual pages from the Linux Documentation Project.

man-db: Manual page reader.

maplay: Plays MPEG-2 audio files in 16 bit stereo.

mawk: Mike's New/Posix AWK Interpreter.

mc: Midnight Commander visual shell.

metamail: Tools and programs for multimedia email.

mgetty: Gert Dring's smart getty replacement for fax (and voice) and data modems. Includes sendfax.

mh: 'mh' mail handling system, with POP support, for use with 'xmh'.

minicom: Minicom, a TTY mode communications package with support for European characters.

mkdosfs-ygg: Creates a DOS FAT filesystem.

mkisofs: Creates a ISO9660 filesystem image, also with Rock-Ridge extensions.

ml: Motif based mail handling programm, supporting pop3d news reading, MIME etc.

modemtool: Configuration tool for /dev/modem.

modules: Utilities for the loadable Linux kernel modules by Bjorn Ekwall and Jaques Gelinas.

moonclock: Traditional oclock with moon phase hacks.

mount: Programs for mounting and unmounting filesystems.

moxfm: Moxfm is a full-fledged file and application manager.

mpage: Places multiple pages of text onto a single postscript page for printing.

mpeg_play: X based player for mpeg files including Red's Nightmare demo.

mt-st: The 'mt' tool allows access to streamer tapes.

mtools: 'mtools' allows access to DOS filesystems.

mule: The Multi-Language Emacs, supports (almost) all languages of the world

multimedia: A CD player and audio mixer for X.

mush: A comfortable interface for electronic mail.

mxp: X mandelbrot set generator and explorer.

ncftp: Ftp client with a nice interface.

ncompress: Extremely fast LZW based file compressor by Peter Jannesen.

ncsa: NCSA HTTP server daemon for providing WWW services.

ncurses: 'ncurses' terminal control library.

ncurses-devel: Development libraries for 'ncurses'.

nenscript: Converts plain ascii to PostScript.

net-tools: Basic network tools e.g. ifconfig, route, ...

netcfg: Network configuration tool.

netpbm: Lots of image conversion and manipulation tools (hpcd support is missing due to a very restrictive redistribution clause).

nfs-server: NFS server daemons.

nfs-server-clients: Client applicationss for use with remote NFS servers.

nis-client: Network Information Service client (formerly yp).

nis-server: Network Information Service server (formerly yp).

nls: Native Language Support (NLS) files for Motif, Netscape, etc.

nvi: New Berkeley vi editor (experimental).

open: Tools for creating and switching between virtual consoles.

optprep: For installing third-party rpm packages such as Caldera's Internet Office Suite..

p2c: Shared library for programs built with the 'p2c' Pascal to C convertor

p2c-basic: A BASIC interpreter based on Pascal using the 'p2c' package.

p2c-devel: Programs and headers for the Pascal to C translator.

pam-apps: Pluggable Authentication Modules (PAM) for Linux.

paradise: Enhanced 'netrek' client with sound and color.

patch: GNU patch Utilities.

pcmcia-cs: PCMCIA Card Services. Tool to support 'hot-swapping' of PCMCIA cards.

pdksh: Public domain korn shell.

perf-rstatd: System monitor using rstatd services (included).

perl: PERL, Practical Extraction and Report Language, Larry Wall's interpreted script language.

perl-add: Practical Extraction and Report Language extensions.

perl-eg: Practical Extraction and Report Language examples.

perl-man: Practical Extraction and Report Language man pages.

perl-pod: Practical Extraction and Report Language documentation.

perl4: Practical Extraction and Report Language (old version).

pidentd: Internet Daemon: Authorization, User Identification.

pine: MIME compliant mail reader with news support as well.

pixmap: X based, comfortable pixmap editor.

plan: Motif based scheduler/planner.

playmidi: Play MIDI files on FM, GUS and MIDI devices.

pmake: Berkeley's parallel make.

pmirror: 'mirror', a perl script for mirroring an FTP site.

popclient: POP – retrieve mail from a mailserver using Post Office Protocol.

portmap: The RPC portmapper daemon.

ppp: 'PPP', Point to Point Protocoll.

printtool: Tool for printer configuration under X (Tcl/Tk based).

procinfo: '/proc' filesystem information.

procmail: 'procmail', a program to filter and process email.

procps: A collection of programs which evaluate the '/proc' structure of the system ('free', 'top', 'uptime' ...).

procps-X11: X based process monitoring utilities.

project-map: The Linux Projects in Progress Map

promondia: Promondia, a Java-based Communication System for the WWW. Supports Chat, Shared Whiteboard and more from within a Web page.

psmisc: More 'ps' type tools for /proc filesystem.

psutils: PostScript Utilities.

python: Very high level scripting language with X interface.

pythonlib: Library of python code used by various Red Hat programs.

rcs: GNU 'rcs' – revision control system.

rdate: Sets the system clock from a network reference. Accurate to about 1 second.

rdist: Remote file distribution client that allows management of identical copies of files on multiple computers.

readline: Library for reading lines from a terminal.

readline-devel: Libraries and header files for developing programs that use the 'readline' library.

recode: Utility for converting textfiles between different fonts according RFC 1345.

rpm: Red Hat Package Manager.

rpm-devel: Header files and libraries for programs that manipulate rpm packages.

rxvt: 'rxvt' – terminal emulator in an X window.

samba: Samba is a Unix based SMB fileserver. It enables a Linux host to become a file and printserver for WfW, OS/2, NT or Windows 95. It also contains a SMB client and a NetBIOS nameserver.

sc: Text based spreadsheet with date support (requires ncurses-devel and bison).

screen: A screen manager with VT100/ANSI emulation, which can be used as a terminal multiplexer operating multiple virtual terminals that can be controlled from one single real terminal.

sed: GNU 'sed' stream editor.

sendmail: Mail transport agent 'sendmail'.

sendmail-cf: 'sendmail' configuration files and m4 macros.

sendmail-doc: 'sendmail' documentation.

setup: Simple setup files

seyon: 'seyon' is a complete X based communication package for modems.

sh-utils: Collection of shell programmers' utilities such as 'basename', 'date', 'dirname', 'expr', 'nohup', 'nice' and 'stty'.

sharutils: GNU shar utils like 'shar', 'unshar', 'uuencode' and 'uudecode'.

slang: Shared library for the C like S-Lang language.

slang-devel: Static library and header files for the C like S-Lang language.

sliplogin: Slip server (derived from BSD 'sliplogin') which works with shadow system and mgetty.

slrn: Small NNTP newsreader.

slsc: Spreadsheet based on 'sc', but with many enhancements.

sox: General purpose sound file conversion tool.

spider: X implementation of the card game Spider.

spray: RPC spray server and client

stat: File information reporter.

statnet: Monitors network traffic in a terminal.

statserial: Displays status of the serial lines in a terminal.

strace: Prints system call trace of a running process.

svgalib: Library for full screen (S)VGA graphics.

svgalib-devel: Development libraries and include files for (S) VGA graphics.

swatch: System log watcher and alarm.

symlinks: Symbolic link sanity checker.

sysklogd: Linux system and kernel logger.

taper: Tape backup system (beta).

tar: GNU tape archiver 'tar'.

tb: Treebrowser is a useful OPEN LOOK (xview) filesystem browser and manager.

tcl: 'Tool Command Language' (tcl) script language.

tcl-devel: 'Tool Command Language' (tcl) script language, development part with man-pages.

tclx: Extensions to 'tcl' and 'tk' for POSIX systems.

tclx-devel: Extensions to 'tcl' and 'tk', development part with man-pages.

tcp_wrappers: Security wrapper for tcp daemons – maximum setting.

tcpdump: 'tcpdump' allows reading and logging of individual TCP/IP packets.

tcsh: 'tcsh', the extended C shell with manual pages.

termcap: Terminal capability collection for GNU libtermcap.

tetex: TeTeX (TeX) typesetting system and MetaFont font formatter.

texinfo: 'texinfo' formatter and info reader.

texinfo-info: Text based standalone 'info' reader.

textutils: GNU text utilities like 'cat', 'cksum', 'head', 'join', 'pr', 'sort', 'split' and 'uniq'.

tgif: Object oriented drawing and construction program with special hyperspace mode.

time: GNU time utility, which allows to determine resource usage such as CPU-time and memory of given program executions.

timetool: RedHat graphical time and date setting tool.

timidity: CPU-intensive renderer for midi music files. Uses only /dev/audio for output but requires (a large set of) sampled instruments in the Gravis Ultrasound's ".pat"-format.

timidity-instruments: set of sampled instruments in the Gravis Ultrasound's ".pat"-format that approximately meets the "General Midi" standard.

tin: 'tin', a news reader with NNTP support.

tix: Collection of many metawidgets, such as notepads, for 'tk'.

tix-devel: Metawidgets for tk, development part with man-pages.

tk: 'Tk' X interface toolkit for 'Tcl'.

tk-devel: 'Tk' toolkit for 'Tcl', development part with man-pages.

tkinfo: Tk/tcl based GNU Info viewer.

tkman: Manual page browser with Tk frontend.

tksysv: X/Tk based System-V 'runlevel' editor.

traceroute: Traces the route that packets take over a TCP/IP network.

tracker: Plays Amiga MOD sound files.

transfig: Converts '.fig' files (such as those from xfig) to other graphic formats.

trn: A threaded news reader with NNTP support.

trojka: A falling blocks game similar to xjewels or tetris for terminals.

tunelp: Configures kernel parallel port driver.

typhoon: Library and utilities for relational databases.

uemacs: MicroEmacs Fullscreen Editor, a small and compact version of Emacs.

umb-scheme: Scheme interpreter from University of Massachusetts at Boston.

umsdos_progs: The programs for the umsdos filesystem, which allows the installation of a Linux system within a DOS partition.

unarj: A decompressor for '.arj' format archives that are widely used under DOS.

units: Units conversion program.

unzip: 'unzip' unpacks '.zip' files such as those made by pkzip under DOS.

usercfg: User and group configuration tool.

util-linux: Various Linux utilities, maintained by Rik Faith.

uucp: Unix to Unix Copy (UUCP) for a mail and news via modem connection. Supports HDB as well as Taylor config files. With extensive documentation and 'uupoll' script from Bodo Bauer.

vga_cardgames: Card games 'klondike', 'oh hell', 'solitaire' and 'spider' the Linux text console.

vga_gamespack: 'othello', 'minesweeper' and 'connect-4' for the linux text console.

vga_tetris: SVGAlib based tetris games.

vim: 'vim' (vi improved), an extended vi editor with support for European characters.

vim-X11: The 'vim' editor (vi improved) with X support.

vixie-cron: The 'cron' daemon allows processes to be started at a predetermined time.

vlock: 'vlock' locks one or more virtual consoles.

vslick: Visual Slick Edit demo version from MicroEdge.

wdiff: GNU word difference finder.

which: Determines which executable would be run based on your PATH variable.

wnn: Common files for all Wnn asian character dictionary servers

wnn-cwnn: Chinese (simplified) character dictionary and server

wnn-devel: Include files and library to compile clients for the Wnn servers

wnn-jwnn: Japanese character dictionary and server

wnn-kwnn: Korean character dictionary and server

wnn-twnn: Chinese (traditional) character dictionary and server

words: English dictionary for ispell.

workman: Graphical (OPEN LOOK) tool for playing audio compact discs including a title management for individual CDs.

woven-docs-LST: Woven Goods Documentation – LST.

woven-docs-RedHat: Woven Goods Documentation – RedHat.

woven-docs-dlhp: Woven Goods Documentation – dlhp.

woven-docs-faq: Woven Goods Documentation – FAQ.

woven-docs-fsstnd: Woven Goods Doc – File System Standard.

woven-docs-howto: Woven Goods Documentation – HOWTO.

woven-docs-isdn: Woven Goods Documentation – ISDN.

woven-docs-ldp: Woven Goods Documentation – LDP.

woven-docs-llhp: Woven Goods Documentation – llhp.

woven-docs-main: Woven Goods Documentation – Main.

woven-docs-usenet: Woven Goods Documentation – UseNet.

woven-docs-wwwhelp: Woven Goods Documentation – WWW Help.

wu-ftpd: Washington University FTP daemon.

x3270: X based 3270 emulator which allows a telnet connection to an IBM host within a X window. Special fonts are used.

xanim: 'xanim' is an animation viewer for X which supports many graphic formats.

xarchie: X based browser interface to 'archie' for querying the world wide archie database archives.

xbill: Kill the Bill.

xbl: 3D Tetris game.

xbmbrowser: Very useful X based browser for bitmaps and pixmaps.

xboard: X11 frontend for GNU Chess.

xboing: Breakout style video game.

xcept-demo: A commercial video text-decoder (BTX/Dx-J) for the X (demo version).

xchomp: PacMan like game for X.

xcolorsel: X based utility to display and select colors from the RGB database.

xdaliclock: An X based 'dali' clock.

xdemineur: Another minesweeper game.

xearth: The earth globe as background for X root.

xemacs-base: XEmacs base package. XEmacs is a powerful, extendable Editor requiring X-libraries but by now also capable of running on plain terminals.

xemacs-emul: Emulation of other editors (mainly vi) for XEmacs.

xemacs-energize: The 'energize' package for XEmacs.

xemacs-hyperbole: The 'hyperbole' package for XEmacs.

xemacs-lispprog: Lisp programming environment for XEmacs.

xemacs-mailnews: Mail and news readers for XEmacs.

xemacs-modes: Miscellaneous special modes for XEmacs.

xemacs-oo-browse: Object browser for XEmacs.

xemacs-packages: Miscellaneous packages for XEmacs.

xemacs-www: WWW browser and editor for XEmacs.

xevil: A fast action explicitly violent game for X.

xf-control-panel: Icon panel with admin tools.

xf-panel: XForms based icon panel with group hierachy.

xfig: Menu driven graphic application for drawing and manipulating objects. It is capable to save objects in various graphic formats.

xfishtank: Turns X root background into an aquarium.

xfm: 'xfm' is a comprehensive file and application manager for X.

xfmail: A spiffy mail reader and editor.

xfractint: Fractal generation program for many different fractal types.

xgalaga: A Galaga clone for X.

xgammon: Backgammon game for one or two players.

xgopher: X based gopher client.

xjewel: A tetris style game for X.

xlander: Moon landing simulation.

xlispstat: Extensible system for statistical computing and dynamic graphics.

xloadimage: X based image viewer supporting many common graphic formats. Images can be displayed or loaded into the background.

xlockmore: X terminal locking program including many screen savers.

xmailbox: X based mail notification tool.

xmbase-grok: A simple data base with graphical X frontend.

xmgr: Motif based plotting tool.

xmine: Mine sweeper for X.

xmorph: A morphing program with an X interface.

xmplay: An X MPEG video viewer.

xntp: 'xntp' allows a precise time synchonisation utilizing a network and/or radio receivers. Requires TCP/IP in the kernel, an initialized loopback device and a correct time zone (see also ktzset from Torsten Duwe).

xosview: An X based utility for viewing the system resources used. For example main memory or cpu load.

xpaint: 'xpaint' is a user friendly program for editing and creating pixmaps and bitmaps.

xpat2: X Patience – various solitaire card games.

xpdf: Portable document format (PDF) viewer for X.

xpilot: Arcade style flying game.

xpm: The Xpm libraries for displaying pixmaps.

xpm-devel: Development libraries and header files for handling of pixmaps.

xpostit: Electronic pinboard for daily dates and important ideas.

xpuzzles: Various geometry puzzles including Rubik's Cube.

xrn: X based news reader.

xscreensaver: X screen savers.

xselection: Utility to get or set an X selection or cutbuffer property value.

xsnow: Xsnow, for those who want Christmas 12 months of the year.

xsysinfo: A performance meter for X.

xtar: Motif based 'tar' tool.

xteddy: The cuddly teddy bear for X – a real must for everyone!

xterm-color: ANSI (color) version of the 'xterm' terminal emulator.

xtetris: X version of tetris.

xtoolwait: Delayed X application launcher.

xtrojka: A falling blocks game similar to xjewels or tetris for X.

xv: Great image viewer/browser for most graphic formats (shareware).

xview: XView library and OpenLook interface for X.

xview-devel: Header files and static libraries for XView application development.

xwatch: A watchdog application for log files.

xwpe: Integrated X-Window programming environment.

xwpick: 'xwpick' is a screen grabber which saves X windows and backgrounds in various formats.

xxgdb: 'xxgdb' is a graphical user interface for the GNU debugger 'gdb'.

ytalk: Uses internet talk protocol to create multiuser chat sessions.

zapem: A space invaders like game.

zgv: Console viewer for many graphics formats.

zip: 'zip', a compression program.

zlib: The un-/compression library zlib.

zlib-devel: Static version and header files for zlib.

zoneinfo: Time zone utilities and data.

zsh: zsh shell.

zz_3dlook: 3D look for all X applications.

The GNU General Public License

The GNU General Public License, abbreviated as GPL, is the basis for the whole Linux system and also for a large part of the software ported to Linux. Through the GPL a software author has the opportunity to make his software available as free software. At the same time his rights and interests are protected by the GPL so that, in contrast to public domain software, he retains a clear copyright and his rights are declared in the license stipulations.

Free software under the GPL

Alongside the GPL there are other license agreements which allow software to be made freely available. FreeBSD and NetBSD, for example, are under the Berkeley Copyright and the X Consortium, from which the X Window system comes, has a special copyright under which this system is made freely available.

Other licence agreements for free software

The term "free" software was coined mainly by Richard Stallman, the author of the famous editor **emacs**. Over 10 years ago he founded the Free Software Foundation (FSF), whose aim is to develop high quality free software.

The Free Software Foundation

To rewrite the GPL in our own words would definitely be the wrong thing to do. Therefore we have printed it here complete and unaltered. Take the time to study the GPL a bit more closely for yourself. Only by doing so will you understand the concepts of free software.

Original version of the GPL

GNU GENERAL PUBLIC LICENSE
Version 2, June 1991

Preamble

The licenses for most software are designed to take away your freedom to share and change it. By contrast, the GNU General Public License is intended to guarantee your freedom to share and change free software–to make sure the software is free for all its users. This General Public License applies to most of the Free Software Foundation's software and to any other program whose authors commit to using it. (Some other Free Software Foundation software is covered by the GNU Library General Public License instead.) You can apply it to your programs, too.

When we speak of free software, we are referring to freedom, not price. Our General Public Licenses are designed to make sure that you have the freedom to distribute copies of free software (and charge for this service if you wish), that you receive source code or can get it if you want it, that you can change the software or use pieces of it in new free programs; and that you know you can do these things.

To protect your rights, we need to make restrictions that forbid anyone to deny you these rights or to ask you to surrender the rights. These restrictions translate to certain responsibilities for you if you distribute copies of the software, or if you modify it.

For example, if you distribute copies of such a program, whether gratis or for a fee, you must give the recipients all the rights that you have. You must make sure that they, too, receive or can get the source code. And you must show them these terms so they know their rights.

We protect your rights with two steps: (1) copyright the software, and (2) offer you this license which gives you legal permission to copy, distribute and/or modify the software.

Also, for each author's protection and ours, we want to make certain that everyone understands that there is no warranty for this free software. If the software is modified by someone else and passed on, we want its recipients to know that what they have is not the original, so that any problems introduced by others will not reflect on the original authors' reputations.

Finally, any free program is threatened constantly by software patents. We wish to avoid the danger that redistributors of a free program will individually obtain patent licenses, in effect making the program proprietary. To prevent this, we have made it clear that any patent must be licensed for everyone's free use or not licensed at all.

The precise terms and conditions for copying, distribution and modification follow.

GNU GENERAL PUBLIC LICENSE TERMS AND CONDITIONS FOR COPYING, DISTRIBUTION AND MODIFICATION

0. This License applies to any program or other work which contains a notice placed by the copyright holder saying it may be distributed under the terms of this General Public License. The "Program", below, refers to any such program or work, and a "work based on the Program" means either the Program or any derivative work under copyright law: that is to say, a work containing the Program or a portion of it, either verbatim or with modifications and/or translated into another language. (Hereinafter, translation is included without limitation in the term "modification".) Each licensee is addressed as "you".

   Activities other than copying, distribution and modification are not covered by this License; they are outside its scope. The act of running the Program is not restricted, and the output from the Program is covered only if its contents constitute a work based on the Program (independent of having been made by running the Program). Whether that is true depends on what the Program does.

1. You may copy and distribute verbatim copies of the Program's source code as you receive it, in any medium, provided that you conspicuously and appropriately publish on each copy an appropriate copyright notice and disclaimer of warranty; keep intact all the notices that refer to this License and to the absence of any warranty; and give any other recipients of the Program a copy of this License along with the Program.

   You may charge a fee for the physical act of transferring a copy, and you may at your option offer warranty protection in exchange for a fee.

2. You may modify your copy or copies of the Program or any portion of it, thus forming a work based on the Program, and copy and distribute such modifications or work under the terms of Section 1 above, provided that you also meet all of these conditions:

   a) You must cause the modified files to carry prominent notices stating that you changed the files and the date of any change.

   b) You must cause any work that you distribute or publish, that in whole or in part contains or is derived from the Program or any part thereof, to be licensed as a whole at no charge to all third parties under the terms of this License.

c) If the modified program normally reads commands interactively when run, you must cause it, when started running for such interactive use in the most ordinary way, to print or display an announcement including an appropriate copyright notice and a notice that there is no warranty (or else, saying that you provide a warranty) and that users may redistribute the program under these conditions, and telling the user how to view a copy of this License. (Exception: if the Program itself is interactive but does not normally print such an announcement, your work based on the Program is not required to print an announcement.)

These requirements apply to the modified work as a whole. If identifiable sections of that work are not derived from the Program, and can be reasonably considered independent and separate works in themselves, then this License, and its terms, do not apply to those sections when you distribute them as separate works. But when you distribute the same sections as part of a whole which is a work based on the Program, the distribution of the whole must be on the terms of this License, whose permissions for other licensees extend to the entire whole, and thus to each and every part regardless of who wrote it.

Thus, it is not the intent of this section to claim rights or contest your rights to work written entirely by you; rather, the intent is to exercise the right to control the distribution of derivative or collective works based on the Program.

In addition, mere aggregation of another work not based on the Program with the Program (or with a work based on the Program) on a volume of a storage or distribution medium does not bring the other work under the scope of this License.

3. You may copy and distribute the Program (or a work based on it, under Section 2) in object code or executable form under the terms of Sections 1 and 2 above provided that you also do one of the following:

Accompany it with the complete corresponding machine-readable source code, which must be distributed under the terms of Sections 1 and 2 above on a medium customarily used for software interchange; or,

Accompany it with a written offer, valid for at least three years, to give any third party, for a charge no more than your cost of physically performing source distribution, a complete machine-readable copy of the corresponding source code, to be distributed under the terms of Sections 1 and 2 above on a medium custom-arily used for software interchange; or,

Accompany it with the information you received as to the offer to distribute corresponding source code. (This alternative is allowed only for noncommercial distribution and only if you received the program in object code or executable form with such an offer, in accord with Subsection b above.)

The source code for a work means the preferred form of the work for making modifications to it. For an executable work, complete source code means all the source code for all modules it contains, plus any associated interface definition files, plus the scripts used to control compilation and installation of the executable. However, as a special exception, the source code distributed need not include anything that is normally distributed (in either source or binary form) with the major components (compiler, kernel, and so on) of the operating system on which the executable runs, unless that component itself accompanies the executable.

If distribution of executable or object code is made by offering access to copy from a designated place, then offering equivalent access to copy the source code from the same place counts as distribution of the source code, even though third parties are not compelled to copy the source along with the object code.

4. You may not copy, modify, sublicense, or distribute the Program except as expressly provided under this License. Any attempt otherwise to copy, modify, sublicense or distribute the Program is void, and will automatically terminate your rights under this License. However, parties who have received copies, or rights, from you under this License will not have their licenses terminated so long as such parties remain in full compliance.

5. You are not required to accept this License, since you have not signed it. However, nothing else grants you permission to modify or distribute the Program or its derivative works. These actions are prohibited by law if you do not accept this License. Therefore, by modifying or distributing the Program (or any work based on the Program), you indicate your acceptance of this License to do so, and all its terms and conditions for copying, distributing or modifying the Program or works based on it.

6. Each time you redistribute the Program (or any work based on the Program), the recipient automatically receives a license from the original licensor to copy, distribute or modify the Program subject to these terms and conditions. You may not impose any further restrictions on the recipients' exercise of the rights granted herein. You are not responsible for enforcing compliance by third parties to this License.

7. If, as a consequence of a court judgment or allegation of patent infringement or for any other reason (not limited to patent issues), conditions are imposed on you (whether by court order, agreement or otherwise) that contradict the conditions of this License, they do not excuse you from the conditions of this License. If you cannot distribute so as to satisfy simultaneously your obligations

under this License and any other pertinent obligations, then as a consequence you may not distribute the Program at all. For example, if a patent license would not permit royalty-free redistribution of the Program by all those who receive copies directly or indirectly through you, then the only way you could satisfy both it and this License would be to refrain entirely from distribution of the Program.

If any portion of this section is held invalid or unenforceable under any particular circumstance, the balance of the section is intended to apply and the section as a whole is intended to apply in other circumstances.

It is not the purpose of this section to induce you to infringe any patents or other property right claims or to contest validity of any such claims; this section has the sole purpose of protecting the integrity of the free software distribution system, which is implemented by public license practices. Many people have made generous contributions to the wide range of software distributed through that system in reliance on consistent application of that system; it is up to the author/donor to decide if he or she is willing to distribute software through any other system and a licensee cannot impose that choice.

This section is intended to make thoroughly clear what is believed to be a consequence of the rest of this License.

8. If the distribution and/or use of the Program is restricted in certain countries either by patents or by copyrighted interfaces, the original copyright holder who places the Program under this License may add an explicit geographical distribution limitation excluding those countries, so that distribution is permitted only in or among countries not thus excluded. In such case, this License incorporates the limitation as if written in the body of this License.

9. The Free Software Foundation may publish revised and/or new versions of the General Public License from time to time. Such new versions will be similar in spirit to the present version, but may differ in detail to address new problems or concerns.

Each version is given a distinguishing version number. If the Program specifies a version number of this License which applies to it and "any later version", you have the option of following the terms and conditions either of that version or of any later version published by the Free Software Foundation. If the Program does not specify a version number of this License, you may choose any version ever published by the Free Software Foundation.

10. If you wish to incorporate parts of the Program into other free programs whose distribution conditions are different, write to the author to ask for permission. For software which is copyrighted by the Free Software Foundation, write to the Free Software Foun-

dation; we sometimes make exceptions for this. Our decision will be guided by the two goals of preserving the free status of all derivatives of our free software and of promoting the sharing and reuse of software generally.

NO WARRANTY

11. BECAUSE THE PROGRAM IS LICENSED FREE OF CHARGE, THERE IS NO WARRANTY FOR THE PROGRAM, TO THE EXTENT PERMITTED BY APPLICABLE LAW. EXCEPT WHEN OTHERWISE STATED IN WRITING THE COPYRIGHT HOLDERS AND/OR OTHER PARTIES PROVIDE THE PROGRAM "AS IS" WITHOUT WARRANTY OF ANY KIND, EITHER EXPRESSED OR IMPLIED, INCLUDING, BUT NOT LIMITED TO, THE IMPLIED WARRANTIES OF MERCHANTABILITY AND FITNESS FOR A PARTICULAR PURPOSE. THE ENTIRE RISK AS TO THE QUALITY AND PERFORMANCE OF THE PROGRAM IS WITH YOU. SHOULD THE PROGRAM PROVE DEFECTIVE, YOU ASSUME THE COST OF ALL NECESSARY SERVICING, REPAIR OR CORRECTION.

12. IN NO EVENT UNLESS REQUIRED BY APPLICABLE LAW OR AGREED TO IN WRITING WILL ANY COPYRIGHT HOLDER, OR ANY OTHER PARTY WHO MAY MODIFY AND/OR REDISTRIBUTE THE PROGRAM AS PERMITTED ABOVE, BE LIABLE TO YOU FOR DAMAGES, INCLUDING ANY GENERAL, SPECIAL, INCIDENTAL OR CONSEQUENTIAL DAMAGES ARISING OUT OF THE USE OR INABILITY TO USE THE PROGRAM (INCLUDING BUT NOT LIMITED TO LOSS OF DATA OR DATA BEING RENDERED INACCURATE OR LOSSES SUSTAINED BY YOU OR THIRD PARTIES OR A FAILURE OF THE PROGRAM TO OPERATE WITH ANY OTHER PROGRAMS), EVEN IF SUCH HOLDER OR OTHER PARTY HAS BEEN ADVISED OF THE POSSIBILITY OF SUCH DAMAGES.

END OF TERMS AND CONDITIONS

Appendix: How to Apply These Terms to Your New Programs

If you develop a new program, and you want it to be of the greatest possible use to the public, the best way to achieve this is to make it free software which everyone can redistribute and change under these terms.

To do so, attach the following notices to the program. It is safest to attach them to the start of each source file to most effectively convey the exclusion of warranty; and each file should have at least the "copyright" line and a pointer to where the full notice is found.

```
<one line to give the program's name and a brief idea of what it does.>
Copyright (C) 19yy <name of author>

This program is free software; you can redistribute it and/or modify
it under the terms of the GNU General Public License as published by
the Free Software Foundation; either version 2 of the License, or
(at your option) any later version.

This program is distributed in the hope that it will be useful,
but WITHOUT ANY WARRANTY; without even the implied warranty of
MERCHANTABILITY or FITNESS FOR A PARTICULAR PURPOSE. See the
GNU General Public License for more details.

You should have received a copy of the GNU General Public License
along with this program; if not, write to the Free Software
Foundation, Inc., 675 Mass Ave, Cambridge, MA 02139, USA.
```

Also add information on how to contact you by electronic and paper mail.

If the program is interactive, make it output a short notice like this when it starts in an interactive mode:

```
Gnomovision version 69, Copyright (C) 19yy name of author
Gnomovision comes with ABSOLUTELY NO WARRANTY; for details type 'show w'.
This is free software, and you are welcome to redistribute it
under certain conditions; type 'show c' for details.
```

The hypothetical commands **show w** and **show c** should show the appropriate parts of the General Public License. Of course, the commands you use may be called something other than **show w** and **show c**; they could even be mouse-clicks or menu items–whatever suits your program.

You should also get your employer (if you work as a programmer) or your school, if any, to sign a "copyright disclaimer" for the program, if necessary. Here is a sample; alter the names:

```
Yoyodyne, Inc., hereby disclaims all copyright interest in the program
'Gnomovision' (which makes passes at compilers) written by James Hacker.

<signature of Ty Coon>, 1 April 1989
Ty Coon, President of Vice
```

This General Public License does not permit incorporating your program into proprietary programs. If your program is a subroutine library, you may consider it more useful to permit linking proprietary applications with the library. If this is what you want to do, use the GNU Library General Public License instead of this License.

Index

Printing and binding: Druckerei Triltsch, Würzburg

Springer
and the
environment

At Springer we firmly believe that an international science publisher has a special obligation to the environment, and our corporate policies consistently reflect this conviction.

We also expect our business partners – paper mills, printers, packaging manufacturers, etc. – to commit themselves to using materials and production processes that do not harm the environment. The paper in this book is made from low- or no-chlorine pulp and is acid free, in conformance with international standards for paper permanency.

 Springer

List of hardware requirements

Linux 2.0 supports almost all common PC hardware. The more widespread a component is the more likely is that problem free useage can be counted upon. Special, brand new and expensive hardware is seldom supported. In doubtful cases Plug & Play should always be disabled. The following overview is by far not complete and only gives a rough guide to hardware support. Only the hardware components required for the installation and graphics cards supported by the graphical interface are listed.

Hardware requirements: Memory: minimum 8MB, recommended 16MB or more
Free harddisk capacity: minimum 50MB, recommended 270-600MB
Bussystem: ISA, VLB, EISA or PCI (not IBM PS/2 and MicroChannel MCA)
Prozessor: Intel/AMD/Cyrix 386SX or better.CDROM drives: SCSI or ATAPI, Aztech CDA268, Orchid CDS-3110, Okano/Wearnes CDD-110, Conrad TXC, GoldStar R420, LMS Philips CM 206, Matsushita/Panasonic, Creative Labs, Longshine, Kotobuki (via Sound-blaster Pro Multi-CD), Mitsumi, Optics Storage Dolphin 8000AT, Sanyo H94A, Sony CDU31A/CDU33A, Sony CDU-535/CDU-531, Teac CD-55A SuperQuad.Harddisk control-lers: IDE, ESDI, EIDE, AMI Fast Disk VLB/EISA.(BusLogic compatible), Adaptec AVA-1505/1515, AHA-1510/152x, AHA-154x, AHA-174x, AHA-274x, AHA-2940/3940, Always IN2000, BusLogic, DPT PM2001, PM2012A, DPT Smartcache (EATA-DMA), DTC 329x, Future Domain TMC-16x0, TMC-3260, TMC-8xx, TMC-950, Media Vision Pro Audio Spectrum 16 SCSI, NCR 5380, NCR 53c400 (Trantor T130B), NCR 53c406a (Acculogic ISApport / Media Vision Premium 3D SCSI), NCR 53c7x0, 53c8x0, Qlogic / Control Concepts SCSI/IDE (FAS408), Seagate ST-01/ST-02, SoundBlaster 16 SCSI-2 (Adaptec 152x compatible), Trantor T128/T128F/T228, UltraStor 14F/24F/34F, Western Digital WD7000 SCSI.

Network cards (Ethernet): 3Com 3C501, 3C503, 3C505, 3C507, 3C509/3C509B, 3C579, 3C589, 3c590, AMD LANCE (79C960), PCnet (AT1500, HP J2405A, NE1500/NE2100), AT&T GIS WaveLAN, Allied Telesis AT1700, Ansel Communications AC3200, Apricot Xen-II, Cabletron E21xx, DEC DE425/DE434/DE435, DEC DEPCA and EtherWORKS, HP PCLAN (27245 and 27xxx series), HP PCLAN PLUS (27247B und 27252A), HP 10/100VG PCLAN, Intel EtherExpress/Pro, NE2000/NE1000, New Media Ethernet, Racal-Interlan NI5210 (i82586 Ethernet chip), Racal-Interlan NI6510 (am7990 lance chip), PureData PDUC8028, PDI8023, SEEQ 8005, SMC Ultra, Schneider & Koch G16, Western Digital WD80x3, Zenith Z-Note / IBM ThinkPad 300 (built in adapter)

Other network cards: ARCnet all ARCnet cards, IBM Tropic chipset cards for Token Ring, Ottawa PI/PI2 & most generic 8530 based HDLC boards for amateur radio (AX.25), SLIP/CSLIP/PPP for serial port, EQL, PLIP for parallel port, AT-Lan-Tec/RealTek & D-Link DE600/DE620 portable adapters

Graphics cards for SVGA mode: VGA, EGA, ARK Logic ARK1000PV/2000PV, ATI VGA Wonder, ATI Mach32, Cirrus 542x, 543x, OAK OTI-037/67/77/87, S3 (limited support), Trident TVGA8900/9000, Tseng ET3000/ET4000/W32

Graphics cards for X (unaccelerated): Tseng (ET3000, ET4000AX, ET4000/W32, ET6000), Western Digital/Paradise PVGA1,Western Digital (WD90C00, WD90C10, WD90C11, WD90C24, WD90C30, WD90C31, WD90C33), Genoa GVGA, Trident (TVGA8800CS, TVGA8900B, TVGA9200CX, TVGA9320, TVGA9400CX, TVGA9420, TGUI9420DGi, TGUI9430DGi, TGUI9440AGi, TGUI9660XGi, TGUI9680), ATI (18800, 18800-1, 28800-2, 28800-4, 28800-5, 28800-6, 68800-3, 68800-6, 68800AX, 68800LX, 88800GX-C, 88800GX-D, 88800GX-E, 88800GX-F, 88800CX, 264CT, 264ET, 264VT, 264VT2, 264GT), NCR (77C22, 77C22E, 77C22E+), Cirrus Logic (CLGD5420, CLGD5422, CLGD5424, CLGD5426, CLGD5428,CLGD5429, CLGD5430, CLGD5434, CLGD5436, CLGD5440, CLGD5446, CLGD5462, CLGD5464, CLGD6205, CLGD6215, CLGD6225, CLGD6235, CLGD6410, CLGD6412, CLGD6420, CLGD6440), OAK (OTI067, OTI077, OTI087), Avance Logic (ALG2101, ALG2228, ALG2301, ALG2302, ALG2308, ALG2401), Chips & Technologies (65520, 65530, 65540, 65545, 65520, 65530, 65540, 65545, 65546, 65548, 65550, 65554),MX (MX68000, MX680010), Video 7/Headland Technologies HT216-32, SiS (86C201, 86C202, 86C205), ARK Logic (ARK1000PV, ARK1000VL, ARK2000PV, ARK2000MT), RealTek RTG3106, Alliance AP6422, Matrox MGA2064W, NVidia/SGS Thomson NV1, STG2000

Graphics cards for X (accelerated): 8514/A (and true clones), ATI (Mach8, Mach32, Mach64), Cirrus Logic (CLGD5420, CLGD5422, CLGD5424, CLGD5426, CLGD5428, CLGD5429, CLGD5430, CLGD5434, CLGD5436, CLGD5440, CGLD5446, CLGD5462, CLGD5464), S3 (86C911, 86C924, 86C801, 86C805, 86C805i, 86C928, 86C864, 86C964, 86C732, 86C764, 86C765, 86C868, 86C968, 86C325, 86C988) Western Digital (WD90C31, WD90C33, WD90C24A) Weitek P9000, IIT (AGX-014, AGX-015, AGX-016), IBM XGA-2 Tseng (ET4000/W32, ET4000/W32i, ET4000/W32p, ET6000) Ark Logic (ARK1000PV, ARK1000VL, ARK2000PV, ARK2000MT) Matrox MGA2064W

Miscellaneous hardware: ISDN (ICN, Teles, Creatix AVM), PCMCIA, serial cards with 8250, 16450, 16550 und 16550A UART's, Pocketadapter (AT-Lan-Tec/RealTek, D-Link DE600/DE620), Iomega Zip drive, most sound cards